A Dram Like This

ALAN REEVE-JONES

A Dram Like This

PRODUCED BY

ELM TREE BOOKS · HAMISH HAMILTON

FOR

WILLIAM GRANT & SONS LIMITED

First published in Great Britain, 1974
by Elm Tree Books Ltd
90 Great Russell Street London WC1
Copyright © 1974 by Alan Reeve-Jones
SBN 241 02277 0

Illustrations by D. A. Mackay

Printed in Great Britain by
Western Printing Services Ltd, Bristol

FOR

HARRY KOVAIRE

AND

THREE SPIRITED COOKS

Contents

Illustrations

FOREWORD

WHISKY is the safest drink in the world—a fact that is being increasingly appreciated everywhere. The author of this admirable introduction to the historical, literary and social associations of *Usquebaugh* (the water of life) is right when he states: 'Whisky is now a wholly universal drink, selling to more than a hundred and seventy countries of the world.' And he is right, too, when he declares that 'whisky is still a product of Scotland and nowhere else'.

Other countries have tried to distil it—without success. The results—in Spain, in Japan, and elsewhere—have indeed been horrible, and have borne no resemblance whatever to the genuine Scottish article.

In recent years I have travelled in many foreign countries, and one of my difficulties has been to find a short drink I can stay on. There is none at all to equal whisky.

Cognac is no substitute; vodka and aquavita are acquired tastes, which no one used to Scotch is likely to acquire. Other short drinks, like absinthe or mastika or slivovitz, cannot be drunk in more than a sample or two without dire consequences.

That is not the case with whisky, and I have drunk it for nearly seventy years without detriment to my constitution. A couple of years ago, I underwent a major operation, and when the doctor came to change my dressings for the last time he sounded me thoroughly and said all my organs were in a condition that would do credit to a man quarter my age, and there was no reason why I shouldn't live to be a hundred!

I always remember another fact about the health-preserving virtues of whisky. In the First World War I served in Salonika for a couple of years. The Salonika affair has been called 'a clubbable war'. There was little real fighting; the main enemy was disease, and the consequent casualties were immensely greater than any incurred on the battlefields.

The principal causes were dysentery, blackwater fever, and malaria. It was noted that when there was whisky in the officers' or sergeants' messes there were few recurrences of malaria, but when whisky was not available the recurrence-rate shot up at once.

Alas, many ships were being sunk in the Mediterranean at the time, and supplies frequently failed to arrive. The Army medical authorities treated malaria with quinine, taken orally or by injection, which caused men's eyesight to be affected and their hair to fall out. Quinine was also expensive.

It would have been cheaper and far more effective to have supplied the sufferers with whisky. But that, of course, was a sensible alternative beyond the Army authorities to contemplate.

'Give a dog a bad name'—and so the widespread prejudice against whisky, inculcated by the Temperance people, prevailed and the death rate steadily increased.

I am not going to take sides in this foreword with one kind of whisky versus another. However, a few years ago malt whisky would not have been available in the majority of pubs—certainly in almost all English pubs. But motoring recently in the Upper Tyne Valley, and coming to lonely little pubs near Falstone or Bewcastle, I found there was no longer this difficulty. All my favourite 'straight malts' were there.

Yet these isolated pubs were only frequented by shepherds, farm-workers and the like. This shows the extent to which the diffusion of the taste for 'pure malt' has increased in recent years to embrace all classes of society.

I have been referring to 'whisky' or 'Scotch', but I am sorry for anyone who asks in a bar for a drink by either of these names instead of nominating the particular brand he wants.

This lack of discrimination entails a great loss of enjoyment. So, too, does the absence of some knowledge of the history and romance of the making and drinking of whisky. A little knowledge of the rich background adds greatly to appreciation of the drink.

That is why I welcome this book. It puts the ordinary drinker in possession of all the main facts, and is, I think, an excellent brief introduction for the general public.

I have said I feel sorry for those who can only ask for 'a whisky' without naming the particular kind they want. But I think this splendid drink deserves to be drunk with due ceremony, whenever possible, and in one of my poems I lament the disappearance of old ritual in this connection:

Not drinking whisky and soda
As an Englishman does, which is very dull,
But with all the splendid old ritual,
The urn, the rummers, the smaller glasses,
The silver ladles, and the main essentials.
The whisky toddy is mixed in a rummer,
A round-bottomed tumbler on a stem,
And transferred at intervals with a silver ladle
Into an accompanying wine-glass
By way of cooling it
Sufficiently for consumption.
Slainte! 'Freedom and whisky gang thegither'. Take aff yer dram!

HUGH MacDiarmid

A DRAM LIKE THIS . . .

WHETHER or not a book about Scotch whisky should be written by a Highlander, imbued with the best kind of prejudice and armed from the genes outwards with some sort of built-in knowledge, must be decided between the reader's love of eulogy and his liking for plain fact. We all have a little Scotch in us, one way or another, and particularly after sundown, but appreciation of the special qualities of Scotland's indigenous spirituous liquor has nothing to do with the nationality of the imbiber. My point of view is that of the recipient, the latter-day customer, remembering that had the stream not flowed south a century or so ago the source might have dried up, parched out of existence by repressive taxation and the mindless vagaries of fashion. That it did not, and instead became a burning torrent, is a piece of good fortune for everyone—including the Scots. Scotch whisky is now a wholly universal drink, selling to more than 170 countries of the world.

The roots of the industry go deep, for it is to the nature of the terrain that the nature of Scotch belongs. The rugged scenery of the hinterland is inherited from some primordial upheaval of the earth's crust, a submarine holocaust of such galvanic violence that rock formations of unimaginable size were forced above the surface of the sea. Afterwards came the ice-flows, decapitating mountains and carving out of barren desolation the first rough outline of today's familiar landscape. Wind and rain brought swift-flowing rivers, and time clothed the bleakness with trees. This evolution over tens of thousands of years in the end provided by glorious accident exactly the right conditions for the making of Scotch whisky. If the 'guid Lord' had a hand in it too we would not be in the least surprised, for the sturdy people of this beleaguered land were given little else for comfort.

Almost every part of Scotland, from the Orkneys to the Lowlands, is geographically suited to the distiller's art, but the richly fertile region immediately south of the Moray Firth ranks first among the natural collecting grounds for the three basic ingredients from which malt whisky, the essential component of all Scotch blends, is prepared. These ingredients are barley, water and peat. Much of the barley is home-grown, but by no means all. Its function is that it should be converted into malt, the result of germination by soaking in water and drying by direct application of heat. The water comes from the sparkling streams that race freely down from distant mountains. The peat may be local or brought from as far away as Fife.

What I have said here suggests that malt whisky can be manu-factured from substances originating outside the area. This is not quite true. The water, by the time it reaches the purlieus of the distillery, is pure, not with the emasculated purity of distilled water, but pure in the sense that it contains chemical and mineral traces of such kind and in such proportion that cannot be artificially reproduced and may not be found elsewhere. There are some who hold that this special character is owed in part to the granite from which the Highland mountains are largely composed, and others, equally sure, who insist that the deciding factor is the physically inimitable make-up of the air drawn into the streams on their way to the distillery. Neither is altogether right, but it is these elements, coupled with a skill in distillation passed down from generation to generation, which give Scotch its subtlety of flavour. Scotch whisky when it reaches the customer, wherever he may be, is still a product of Scotland and of nowhere else.

I

FROM THE MISTS OF ANTIQUITY

THE earliest ancestor of malt whisky was probably a distillation from barley made by the ancient Egyptians. There is no written history, but a few classical allusions suggest that the art may have been taken up by the Greeks, following the conquest of Egypt by Alexander the Great in the years between 332 and 323 B.C.

The word 'alcohol' is itself of Arabic origin, coming from *al-koh'l* which in turn derives from *kohl*, the metallic substance used by Islamic women, then as now, to beautify the eyelids. The literal translation is 'the staining powder'. Its application is to anything that is highly refined, therefore the term lent itself naturally to distillates. The irony remains that Islamic peoples are forbidden by their religion to touch it.

It may be supposed that the Arab chemists well understood that one of the properties of alcohol was that the effect on the human system could be to intoxicate and that in circumstances of its being prepared from certain ingredients it could also blind and kill. A method the Greeks took away with them was for the preparation of what they called barley wine, a distillation or brewage from barley which functioned only as a drink and could scarcely be broken down again for the making of medicines and perfume. It was not until after the death of Mohammed in A.D. 630 that the strict injunctions of the Koran disallowed the drinking of alcohol to adherents of the Moslem faith. The spread of Mohammedanism was immediate and of immense power. Warring tribes were welded into one nation, free of race prejudice but intent on carrying the Word of the Prophet to all corners of the earth by force. In less than a hundred years the fanatical Islam empire had encompassed the whole of the Middle East, North Africa, the north of India, and even Spain. And without a drop to drink.

If the reader wonders what all this has to do with whisky, let me remind him that had the Muslim wave of conquest not been stopped in France in A.D. 732, there might never have been such a thing as Scotch whisky and all of us, including the Scots, would still be drinking sherbet.

As it happened, the inquiry into distillation processes continued steadily through the centuries. Wine-making had been known and studied since Man ceased to be nomadic and became a farmer. It is reasonable to suspect that the first wine happened accidentally. Yeast appears on grapes as they ripen, for no known cause. This is a natural yeast, which attacks the sugar in the juice when grapes are pressed. In our hypothetical case a few ripened grapes will have fallen into a shallow rock-pool exposed to hot sunlight. Fermentation carries on, releasing carbon dioxide, and turning the water into wine. Weak, coarse wine indeed—but wine. We must also imagine a shepherd, thirsty from the heat, cupping his hands and drinking from this miraculous pool. Having tried it once he tries it again—and not being an idiot he sees what has happened. Dionysus, the god of wine, also called Bacchus by both Greeks and Romans, was not a pastoral god for nothing. He was worshipped by humble folk whom wandering bands of ecstatic admirers brought into Greece from Thrace in the eighth century B.C. The cult which developed was characterised by a mystic frenzy when these followers, pleasantly muddled with wine, identified themselves with Dionysus—or the shepherd-inventor of this astonishing new drink—and hurried unsteadily home to tell their friends. And this was only wine. Distilled spirit came later.

Mediaeval alchemists played a great part in improving the systems of extracting the alcoholic essences from grain, although not always to produce beverages. Albertus Magnus, the thirteenth-century philosopher, left an account of how to produce what he called *aqua ardens*, or 'burning water', by distillation, but most of the savants of the Middle Ages were concerned with the breaking down of flowers and herbs for medicinal use and in the making of perfumes. Sometimes they distilled and re-distilled in the hope of discovering the ultimate panacea, the final nostrum against all ills, and found—alcohol. Another thirteenth-century alchemist who studied and wrote about distilling was the Spanish philosopher Raymond Lull, referred to by Professor David Daiches in his immensely erudite book *Scotch Whisky, its Past and Present*.

During these formative years it is certain that the experimenters will have had little experience of the dangers that go with the drinking of supposedly potable spirit made from distillations other than of grain or fruit. The bridge between the 'water of life' and the 'waters of Lethe' is narrow. (If I may digress for a moment, I will explain that alcohols are a class of organic compounds of general formula $R-OH$, where R is an aliphatic radical. The word 'aliphatic' describes derivations of hydrocarbons having chains of carbon atoms, as distinct from rings of carbon atoms as in benzene. These factors are differently constituable. Ethyl alcohol, or ethanol, is produced by distilling fermented liquors and is safe for human consumption. Methyl alcohol, or methanol, can be obtained by distilling wood and is a poison.)

Drinking for pleasure, contrary to drinking for medicinal reasons, was the privilege only of the wealthy in mediaeval France, until improved methods of distillation, using the early pot-still—where heat is applied directly and not by steam jacket—led to the beginning of a manufacturing industry able to serve the needs of a wider range of consumers.

By the early seventeenth century the poor in France were

drinking rough native wines and the rich the brandies distilled from these same wines by alchemists and monks and often by skilled retainers whose work was to maintain the supplies at a constant level.

Varieties of spirits, other than brandies, developed throughout Europe, but grain-based spirits were less successful. Benedictine, the great French liqueur, dates from 1510, and is still made from a secret formula in the monastery at Fécamp. Cognac, named after the district, is double-distilled in much the same way as malt Scotch whisky and similarly needs long maturing. Armagnac, single-distilled, is sometimes aged for twenty years. In the seventeenth century the Carthusian order of monks invented Chartreuse, a distillation involving some 130 herbs, in the Grenoble area. Throughout Europe, including England, the spirit drink of the titled and landed classes was based on the grape, until, a little over a century ago, the totally unexpected disaster that came through the accidental introduction of the Phylloxera aphid wiped out the vines and almost closed down the industry. Within twenty years this tiny parasite, brought over with an importation of American vines, had virtually destroyed the work of centuries. But ill winds have a way of blowing good. The gap in the market was filled by Scotch whisky, a triumph from which brandy was never to recover.

When the Highlanders first produced whisky proper is not known. The original discoverers may have been Picts, the pre-Celtic inhabitants of the extreme north and north-east, or, as is more probable, the Scots, who came from Ireland in the fifth century A.D. and occupied the greater part of the country. Quite certainly these Celtic invaders had been making a spirituous drink from unmalted barley and other grains from a very long time before. The generic Irish brought with them their Gaelic language, the Christian religion, and the tribal name by which this new colony was to be known. It is therefore logical to assume that they may have brought with them the skills of whisky distilling as well. Even the word 'whisky' derives from the Gaelic variation of the Celtic *uisge beatha*. John Doxat in his masterly *Drinks and Drinking* lines it up in this way: aqua vitae

—*uisge beatha*—usquebaugh—usky—wusky—whiskey—whisky. One has to admit that this sounds just a little like someone trying to remember what he wants a few seconds before closing time. But to revert: Most writers on the subject accept that Scotch whisky came from Irish whiskey (with an 'e'), beloved of the Christian missionary monks and manufactured by them on settlements progressively heading from the west coast into central Scotland.

Changes in the method of production presumably came with the adoption of malting. Even so, I once met an old crofter who insisted that the whole process was the discovery of the Picts already mentioned, the original 'little people' of legend, and stolen from them by marauding Irish pirates, together with, but taking precedence over, sheep and women—in that order.

The first reference to a spirit distilled from barley in Scotland, quoted by every student of distilling, occurs in the Scottish Exchequer Rolls of 1494, with an entry of 'eight bolls of malt to Friar John Cor wherewith to make aquavitae'. Nothing more is recorded of the next ten years, but home distilling must by this time have become widespread, for in 1505 a measure of control was imposed from Edinburgh by giving supervisory powers over manufacture to the then newly-formed Royal College of Surgeons. The Worshipful Company of Distillers was formed by doctors for a similar purpose in the reign of Charles the First.

King James IV of Scotland (1488–1513) was known to have been provided with aqua vitae at Inverness in 1506, probably from a local farmstead, and the earliest reference to a distillery in the Acts of the Scottish Parliament appeared in 1699, with mention of the Ferintosh distillery owned by Duncan Forbes of Culloden. In his book *Scotch*, Sir Robert Bruce Lockhart points out that of Culloden itself the tragic defeat of the Jacobites in 1746 in fact opened the Highlands to the Lowlands and the road to the south for Highland whisky.

II

THE MIDDLE YEARS

'With usquebae we'll face the deevil.'

—ROBERT BURNS, 1759–96

THE story of Scotch really begins with the English attempt to subjugate the defeated followers of Prince Charles, and indeed the whole country, after the 1745 rising. It was to be a system of punishment by repression combined with the practical object of raising money by taxation. As far back as 1644 an excise duty on spirits had been imposed by the Scots Parliament. Like the earlier impost it proved impossible to collect; crofts were generally remote and usable roads almost non-existent. But after Culloden an army of excisemen, known locally as 'gaugers' —and strangely Robert Burns was later to become one—set about combing the Highlands for illicit stills, supported by the military and officials appointed to enforce legislation. Severe penalties including transportation went with the carrying of arms, and the wearing of the kilt was prohibited.

The immediate effect of these restrictions was to foment so

powerful a feeling against injustice that a nation of small farmers, already disrupted by war and the severance of old loyalties, formed itself into an interlacing network of free traders. More than 200 illicit stills sprang up in the Glenlivet–Tomintoul area. Independent and later concerted smuggling became almost a respectable form of trade, often involving the minister and the laird as deeply in the conspiracy as the farmer. The motive was by no means only monetary gain; the Highlanders were determined that the hated English should not suppress one of the last vestiges of Gaelic civilisation. To the Scotsman whisky was no less a national drink than a commercial product of the land he worked, like his oatmeal and livestock. The taxes imposed on legitimate distilling, if collected, could easily turn a meagre profit into loss, and this in the ferocious northern winter meant starvation. Another factor, making some of the English almost tolerable again, was that the conqueror had acquired a taste for the fiery spirit of the Scots and willingly bought it—south of the Border.

The Government's answer was to charge an import duty of 9s. 6d. a gallon, the first of many fiscal blows to come.

In 1814 distillation in stills of less than 500 gallons was prohibited. An obvious consequence was that smuggling increased to a point where by 1823 more than half the whisky sold came from the small illicit stills.

The best malt whisky was, and is, produced in the Speyside district, a belt of land bounded on the west by the River Ness and on the east by the River Deveron. Each man to his taste, of course, but the majority of malt distilleries of Scotland are here for a reason. In deference to those whose opinions differ, it must be stated clearly that splendid whiskies also come from areas far distant from the Speyside belt. The malt whiskies are divided into four groups according to the geographical location of the distilleries in which they are made, as follows:

1. Highland malt whisky, made north of an imaginary line from Dundee on the east to Greenock on the west.
2. The Lowland malt whiskies, made south of the line.
3. Islays, from the island of that name.

4. Campbeltowns, from the town of that name in the Mull of
   Kintyre.

At the end of the seventeenth century and early in the
eighteenth the new contraband trade made for competition
between the distillers, which greatly improved the quality. But
these same opportunities encouraged distillers in the Lowlands
to market an inferior product, with Edinburgh as its centre.
With or without taxation the whisky made here was cheap to
concoct and cheap to buy. Over the next hundred years the
contraband in raw and dubious spirit reached so low a standard
that Scotch whisky imported into England was more often than
not redistilled and flavoured for turning into gin.

By 1820, fine single malts were being made illicitly in all parts
of the Highlands and often equally fine whiskies were legally
being produced by firms of which many were made bankrupt
because of taxation. Spurious whiskies, based on rye and even
wheat with barley, were selling successfully in England and
quickly replacing ale as the new basic alcoholic drink of the
Lowlands. Smuggling in both varieties was rife.

To restore the status of Highland whisky to its past eminence,
the 4th Duke of Gordon, the largest landowner in the Central
Highlands, raised the matter in the House of Lords. He proposed that if the Government would sanction the manufacture
of legal whisky of a quality equal to the illicit's on payment of a
reasonable duty, he and other Highland landowners would try
to suppress the widespread and well-organised activities of the
smugglers.

The proposal was approved, and the Act of 1823 sanctioned
legal distilling on payment of a duty of 2s. 3d. a gallon proof
spirit and a licence of £10 for all stills with a capacity of forty
gallons and over. Good whisky now had a chance to oust the
firewater compounded in the Lowland cities.

This was by no means the end of illicit distilling in Scotland,
which was carried on at a diminishing rate for the next sixty
years, but it was certainly the beginning of Scotch whisky as an
organised industry.

In 1822, before the Act was ratified, King George IV paid a

state visit to Scotland and gave the trade a considerable fillip
by insisting on drinking whisky while he was there. As it happened the particular kind he demanded was Glenlivet, of which
there was none in Edinburgh at the time, but with difficulty and
a good deal of artful connivance a private bin of genuine contraband Glenlivet was brought to Holyrood and presented to His
Majesty, who, in full Highland dress, kilt and all, was graciously
pleased to accept it. He had been on the throne for two years,
and much of the fire had gone out of him since his Regency days,
but what was good for the King was good for the Court—and
good for business.

One of the first holders of a licence under the 1823 Act, as
Bruce Lockhart relates, was a young Glenlivet farmer called
George Smith. He was well educated and had been trained as an
architect, for no one could possibly foresee the part he was to
play in the future of whisky distilling. When his father died,
leaving him the farm at Upper Drumin, near the village of
Glenlivet itself, he not only operated the existing illicit still there
but took a leading part in the dangerous game of hoodwinking
the excisemen and running contraband down to the merchants
in the Lowlands.

This was far too crude a method of trading for a man of
Smith's calibre. As soon as distilling on payment of a fee was
sanctioned, he changed his coat and became licensed. It was not
an easy decision to make, for his neighbours and confederates
were bitterly opposed to what they believed was the Duke of
Gordon's interference in profitable local affairs. The feeling
against the English had moderated dramatically in the last forty
years, but any proposed legislation, even if helpful, could only
exacerbate old wounds.

His companions now turned against George Smith, whom
they regarded as a blackleg. The Glenlivet Distillery, which had
at once come into existence, was threatened with burning.
Bands of angry freebooters lay in wait for its whisky convoys.
But the pioneer of lawful trading under the Act was not to be
deterred. He was shrewd enough to see that the buccaneering
days were over and courageous enough to withstand the violence

of his former friends. The ethics of the matter did not concern him; he evolved new principles, which after twelve years of fierce opposition brought peace to the glen and opened the way to a lasting rapport with the consumer.

III

THE ASCENDANCY OF GRANT'S
'Freedom and whisky gang thegither.'
—ROBERT BURNS

WILLIAM GRANT & SONS LTD is the largest independent firm of whisky distillers in the world and as much a family concern as it was when it started.

The Grant reputation for individuality and enterprise was soundly established in the Highlands long before the emergence of distilling as an industry, and might indeed have been achieved in quite a different way. The story can be taken up from 16 April 1746, the date of Culloden. Three of the survivors were brothers —Alexander, Daniel and William Grant. Alexander, the eldest, was already known as Auld Cearnach, either because the brothers came from Glen Cearnach or more probably because the word means 'hero' or 'freebooter' in Gaelic. 'Freebooter' is a corruption of the Dutch *vrijbuiter*, a smuggler, and when we remember that so-called 'illicit' distilling had been going on honourably in Scotland since 1644, the sobriquet may have had a particular significance. This we do not know, but what we do know is that all three brothers became farmers—perhaps because they were farming people before taking up arms against George II.

Alexander lived to a great age (he is said to have been 103 when he died), but it was the youngest brother, William, whose adventurous spirit took him completely away from the hard life on the land and found him at fifty competing with experienced industrialists in the Lancashire cotton trade. Iron determination to succeed was suitably rewarded, for within a generation his sons gained immortality as the originals of the Cheeryble brothers in Charles Dickens's *Nicholas Nickleby*.

This breakaway was not copied by Auld Cearnach's son—also named Alexander—who continued to tend his father's farm at Bellahourn until his untimely death at thirty-seven. The second Alexander had left behind him a large family, one of whom, William Grant, was born in January 1784. As the living was arduous, and perhaps because this young man was so lacking in physical stature he might have been thought a weakling, it was decided that he should become a tailor. He was therefore apprenticed to a brother already qualified in the tailoring trade and served his time with him. But this was no occupation for a Grant. Not this one, anyway. With the coming of the Napoleonic Wars, William enlisted in the First Battalion the Ninety-Second Regiment of Foot, later to be called the Gordon Highlanders, and served overseas through its many campaigns leading up to the final victory.

On his discharge at Newcastle in 1817, he walked the 320 miles to Dufftown, a mere stroll to a man who had been through what he had been through, and became known for the rest of his days as 'Old Waterloo'. Auld Cearnach would have been proud of him. He married twice, and by his second wife, Elizabeth Reid, became the father of still another William Grant, on 19 December 1839—the one destined to surpass in achievement all the others of his line.

There was to be little schooling for this William, herding had to come first; but the seeds of ambition were implanted at childhood. Again because farming scarcely made a living for those engaged in it, his parents put him to work as a trainee shoemaker. It was a failure. William Grant already knew himself to possess qualities of personal capability and leadership far beyond the average and could not be content with a job offering such slender prospects. He secured a post as clerk at the Tininiver lime works at Crachie. This was a good step up, but the drive within him was still not satisfied. With hopes of rising to be a manufacturer of lime on his own account, he made a comprehensive study of the lime deposits in the north of Scotland and on one occasion walked to Balmoral and back in two days, a distance of 120 miles, to examine the possibilities of opening up there. In the end he made up his mind to quarry for limestone on the outcrops near Dufftown itself, and, after inquiring thoroughly into the availability of the site, made detailed plans for the building of kilns on the laird's estate. At the last moment the promised concession was refused.

It was following this setback that William Grant's career in whisky really began. He was twenty-seven. Like all Highlanders he had the makings of a distiller already in his blood, and when the opportunity offered he took over as bookkeeper, and later manager, at Mortlach Distillery, then owned by Messrs Gordon & Cowie.

The quality of patience is vital to the making of malt whisky, as it is to those who engage in it. William had to wait another twenty years before he could leave Mortlach and set up at last, having garnered a complete knowledge of distilling and distillery construction, as head of his own business.

The chance came in the summer of 1886. The owner of Cardow Distillery, a woman, decided to install new plant; the old was for sale and William Grant was able to buy it for £119 19s. 10d. The saving of the money had been immensely difficult, for pay at Mortlach had necessarily been poor (these were hard times for everyone in Scotland) and there had been seven sons and three daughters to bring up. Fortunately, the boys were all imbued with the Grant determination to get on, and as the site for the distillery had long been chosen, the work of building could now begin. This is not to say that the girls did not play their part, but history records that the labour was completed by William and his sons in under a year. The first whisky ran from the stills of Glenfiddich Distillery on Christmas Day, 1887.

Had this been the family's only accomplishment it would have been remarkable enough, but time was somehow found for other pursuits. Grant had always had an inclination towards bookishness and wanted his children to reach the heights of education his own early penury had denied him. These hopes were fully realised. With less than £100 a year coming in to feed and clothe ten children, William Grant had managed to send five of his sons to university. A supervisor from the Customs and Excise, on his first visit to the Glenfiddich plant, was astounded to see students' textbooks lying around in the distillery, the property of the still man, the malt man, and the tun man—who became, respectively, Dr Alexander Grant, Dr George Grant, and, in the case of Charles Grant, a Captain in the army and eventually, as part of a long-term plan, the owner of Glendronach Distillery.

The foresight and hard work of the family team was to find its own reward. The enterprise flourished from the start, for the whisky was of fine quality, due severally to the expert knowledge the senior Grant had gained as a manager, the climatic and geographical perfection of the site's location, and the character and purity of the Robbie Dubh spring which supplied the plant. Today the soft crystal-clear water from this spring still originates with the clean melting snows on the slopes of the Conval hills overlooking the village of Dufftown, and is conveyed through a piping system to a reservoir holding 100,000 gallons.

In 1890, four years after building Glenfiddich, William Grant and his sons bought for £200 the new Balvenie Castle, a derelict eighteenth-century mansion, a little further down the glen, and converted it into a second distillery. Balvenie is now the name of a straight malt of Grant's on sale in bottle to the public but

GLENFIDDICH DISTILLERY

A COOPER MAKING
A CASK AT THE
GLENFIDDICH
DISTILLERY

POTSTILLS

THE GIRVAN AND LADYBURN DISTILLERY

principally used in blending. The change from Grant's operating only as distillers and becoming blenders, wholesalers and exporters took place in 1898. This followed the sensational crash of Pattisons Ltd, a firm of blenders in Leith. Initially successful, because the whisky trade was at last beginning to boom, brothers Robert and Walter Pattison plunged recklessly into the business of setting up new distilleries indiscriminately. The effect was that production soon exceeded the demand, and the bottom fell out of the whisky market.

The Pattison failure had a lamentable backlash for the whole trade and many distillers were made bankrupt, but three months before the collapse, as though warned by second sight, William and his son John had cut back on production. William's son-in-law, Charles Gordon, then the headmaster of Cabrach, a local school in Upper Banffshire, was brought into the firm because of old associations with the family and sent to Glasgow to establish the blend of 'Stand Fast'—the war-cry of Auld Cearnach and the men of Clan Grant at Culloden.

Charles's one-man campaign was not immediately successful. Indeed, it took him 181 calls to sell the first case, and after 503 calls it was still only one. But confidence in the product and a sturdy refusal to accept defeat were soon to be rewarded; customers acknowledged the excellence of the blend and sales on the home market gradually began to rise. In 1904, John Grant went abroad to establish agencies in Canada and the United States; and in later years the indefatigable Charles Gordon again and again made pioneering trips to the Far East. Progress was now to be steady, for all the delays brought by the 1908 Royal Commission to the settling of the 'What is Whisky?' question, the hazards of competition, the punitive taxes imposed by Lloyd George, and near Prohibition throughout the First World War.

William Grant died in 1923 in his eighty-fourth year. His portrait hangs in the London office of William Grant & Sons Ltd, and reveals, as Bruce Lockhart puts it: 'a fine old warrior with moustache and mutton-chop whiskers and wearing the full Highland uniform of a major.'

Beneath the portrait is the following verse:

> Lord grant guid luck tae a' the Grants,
> Likewise eternal bliss,
> For they should sit among the sa'nts
> That make a dram like this.

IV

THE PATH OF DUTY

'Dearest of distillation! Last and best! How art thou lost!'
—*Parody on Milton:* ROBERT BURNS

ANYTHING that happens too quickly or too easily in commerce is likely to arouse suspicion in the official as well as the public mind. After the Phylloxera débâcle on the Continent, the French, in a hurried attempt to hold their cognac markets, exported in quantity to this country cognac blended with much inferior spirits. In 1904 the Borough Council of Islington brought proceedings under the Food and Drugs Act against certain public houses for offering for sale brandy which was 'not of the nature, substance and quality of the article demanded by the purchaser.' The prosecutions were successful.

The turn of whisky was to arrive a year later. In Liverpool a charge similar to the Islington one was laid concerning a bottle of whisky labelled 'Pure Malt Pot Still', which was found by the public analyst to be of equal parts of malt, or pot-still spirit, and grain, or patent-still spirit—by any standards a very satisfactory proportioning. But the offence had been an instance of improperly representing the fluid content of the bottle to be pure malt pot-still whisky, which it was not. The case was found proved, and a fine of 20s., plus costs, was imposed.

Again summonses were taken out by Islington Borough Council, and the magistrate of the North London Police Court, before whom one of the cases was heard, gave judgement against the defendants; which meant this time that patent-still whisky was not true whisky and that blends containing it had been subject to adulteration in terms of the Food and Drugs Act.

The decision was a serious setback to the Distillers Company Ltd, an increasingly powerful amalgamation since its inception in 1887, and the Scotch blended-whisky trade generally. There was an appeal, but the bench was divided and so the earlier judgement had to stand.

The malt distillers felt that a moral victory had been won over their rivals the newcomer grain distillers and blenders, but later it was to become apparent that neither of the two main divisions of Scotch whisky distilling could prosper without the other.

Firstly there had to be a lawful definition of the term 'whisky'. It was decided that the influential D.C.L. should ask the President of the Board of Trade to appoint a Committee, or a Royal Commission, to settle the vexed question once and for all. 'What is Whisky?' became the popular name of the intricate and laboured inquiry which followed.

After thirty-seven sittings and the examination of 116 witnesses, visits to distilleries in Scotland, Ireland, and even some brandy distilleries in France, the Commission's final report was published. The tables were turned, for the report contained the phrase: 'we are unable to recommend that the use of the word "whiskey" should be restricted to spirit manufactured by the pot-still process.' It also said:

Our general conclusion, therefore, on this part of our inquiry is that 'whiskey' is a spirit obtained by distillation from a mash of cereal grains saccharified [i.e. turned into sugar] in the diastase of malt; that 'Scotch Whiskey' is whiskey, as above defined, distilled in Scotland; and that 'Irish Whiskey' is whiskey, as above defined, distilled in Ireland.

The victory, however, was not absolute. No victory ever is. With the advent of the First World War, and the cutting off of yeast supplies from Europe, together with the real danger of workers' efficiency being impaired by alcohol, the British Government seriously considered imposing prohibition on the whole country. The move, sponsored by Lloyd George, Chancellor of the Exchequer, was prevented by William Ross, then Managing Director of D.C.L. and founder of Scotch Malt Distillers Ltd as well as the United Yeast Co. Ltd, who successfully presented the argument that the manufacture of yeast was as vital to the baking of the country's bread as was the distilling of alcohol for industrial and military use. Lloyd George, a fanatical opponent of strong drink, compromised by supporting the Immature Spirits (Restriction) Act, which forbade delivery of whisky for consumption in Britain unless it had matured in a bonded warehouse for not less than three years.

This Act, like many others intended only as a wartime measure, has remained in force ever since. Its effect was to reduce drastically the sale of cheap raw spirit to the public and ensure that all brands released on the market were to some extent of a guaranteed maturity. For the first time a restrictive practice was to be of benefit to the industry, in quality if not in quantity, although no evidence of this was to be seen for many years. By 1917 distilling ceased altogether. The price of whisky went up astronomically, and many of the smaller blending and distributing firms went out of business. The grain distillers in the D.C.L. group produced industrial alcohol for war purposes and the independent malt distillers, because of limitations imposed by their different system of manufacture, did not. In the immediate post-war years a great number of these independents, of which William Grant & Sons Ltd was a notable exception, agreed to amalgamation proposals made by D.C.L.

The false boom of the early 1920s, followed by a deliberate reduction in output, increased duty, and the tottering of the nation's economic stability, reduced consumption by half. Quality remained high, but the availability of money, coupled with the total withdrawal of America from the international market, presented the Scotch whisky industry as a poor invest-ment. In England alone the overall production figures had fallen from 16·9 million gallons in 1912–14 to a little over 8 million in 1929–30. Scotland's home consumption fell by nearly two-thirds. But worse was to follow.

The Second World War repeated the disasters of its predeces-sor. Cereals held by D.C.L. were requisitioned. Distillers were informed that the production of whisky would cease at the end of 1939. This would have meant a complete close-down and probably the dissolution of many more firms within the structure of the trade had not three short periods of distilling been allowed for export. Rationing on the home market began in 1940. 1,200,000 gallons of whisky were lost in the same year when a warehouse of the Caledonian Distillery in Edinburgh was hit by a bomb. In other raids a further 3,500,000 proof gallons were destroyed. In April 1945, Mr Churchill gave the instruction:

> On no account reduce the barley for whisky. This takes years to mature, and is an invaluable export and dollar producer. Having regard to all our other difficulties about exports, it would be most improvident not to preserve this characteristic British element of ascendancy.

So it came about, exports flourished with the ending of the war, and from 1947 to 1953 the home consumer had to make do with the allocation allowed by an agreement between the Ministry of Food, the Board of Trade and the Scotch Whisky Association. The quota system ceased in 1954 and rationing imposed by the distillers themselves was lifted in 1959. Success has since been the keynote of the Scotch whisky industry, and annual assets now have a value totalling £250 million.

V

THE STORY OF MALT

THE chemical, physical and engineering processes that go to the making of Scotch whisky are, of course, complex; so much so that to expound them properly would call for expert knowledge and a familiarity with technical terms I do not possess. Instead, I shall try to explain the general system of manufacture as it was explained to me, simply and without embellishment. When a recruit joins the army, he is told: 'This is a rifle. The bullet goes in here—like this—and it comes out of the other end when you pull the trigger. Like that.' The instructor says nothing about expanding gases, velocity, or heat absorption. Perhaps, like me, he knows his limitations. Very well, then. Let's just pull the trigger.

There are two kinds of Scotch whisky: *malt whisky* which is prepared from malted barley only, and *grain whisky* made from malted barley together with unmalted barley and maize. Malt or grain whiskies coming from one distillery are known as single whiskies. The combining of malt with malt or grain with grain is called 'vatting'; not to be confused with the combining of whiskies from several different distilleries, malt as well as grain, for which the term 'blending' is used. Most of the whiskies retailed are blends.

But first must come the traditional pot-still malt Scotch whisky made from barley; in the past, and to a large extent today, a division of the normal routine of a farming community. The barley need not be local, but to produce malt of the desired quality it must be fully ripened, dry, and of the needed protein content.

The first stage of malting is the 'steeping' of the barley by regular adding and draining of water sufficient to bring the moisture content up to 44 per cent, to encourage germination and to give 'life' to the barley during its time on the malting floor. After steeping, the barley is dropped to the floor beneath, where it is couched in a deep pile to promote germination before being further spread on the floor where it will be turned regularly to avoid overheating. During this period on the floor, normally eight to ten days, the grain undergoes certain chemical changes which transform the contents of the seed of grain into maltose (a form of sugar). When this stage is reached the malt is put into the drying kiln where the growing process is arrested. (It has not however been killed off and will become active again in the mashing process.)

It is here in the drying kiln that peat enters the process. Hot air and smoke from a peat fire are drawn up through a depth of one to three feet of grain spread across a floor of wire mesh. Peat was once the only fuel used, but nowadays coke or anthracite is substituted after about twenty-four hours and the temperature is slowly raised until only a tiny quantity of moisture remains.

The malted grain from the kiln is now down to 4 per cent moisture content and too hard to permit easy extraction of the sugar. It is therefore passed through a crushing mill and reduced to grist (60 per cent meal, 30 per cent husk and 10 per cent flour).

The grist is passed to the mash-tun and is introduced to hot water at 154°F and it is during this process, assisted by the rakes (stirrers) of the mashing machine, that the conversion takes place. That is to say the starches are converted to soluble sugars. The mixture is then left to infuse for another forty-five minutes, the resulting liquid being slowly drained off and passed through the underback to the heat exchange unit where it loses about 100°F to the cold water arriving for the next process. There are in all three waters taken off—the first and second are destined for future fermentation and the third, which contains only a small quantity of sugar, is retained for the next process. The cooled worts is then passed to the tun room and fed into a large tun, probably one of several capable of holding up to 10,000 gallons. Yeast is pumped in at the same time. (Yeast contains powerful enzymes which promote fermentation.) The effect is to produce, by continuous action, alcohol and carbon dioxide. After thirty-six to forty hours of turbulence a clear brownish liquid known as the wash results, which consists of water, yeast, and a little over 5 per cent by volume of alcohol. The worts has been changed by brewing into a crude form of beer.

What happens now, even in the most modern of distilleries, is intrinsically no different from the traditional method employed for hundreds of years in the making of Highland malt Scotch whisky. It requires not less than two bulbous copper stills, called pot-stills, in which the liquid is turned into vapour and then condensed back into liquid again. The first of these is the wash still. Heat is applied, either by open flame or piped steam, and the wash reaches boiling point. Since alcohol boils at a lower point than the other contents of the wash it comes off first in the form of vapour. The vapour then passes up the neck of the still and down to a coiled copper pipe, the worm, which is immersed in a tank of cold water. The function of this pipe is to hold the vapour until the lower temperature produced by the surrounding cold water makes it condense, as I have said, back into liquid which passes through a spirit safe (35 per cent by volume is retained).

The whole operation is now repeated in the second pot-still.

The liquid, under the title of low wines, again 35 per cent by volume, passes through a second spirit safe, containing a hydrometer for measuring the specific gravity. At the conclusion of the second distillation, via a worm as before, the gross impurities have been deflected and the acceptable spirit (not to be termed whisky for at least three more years) goes into the spirit receiver and on into oak casks for the long years of maturing in the warehouses.

All I have given is a rough outline, for the object is not just to produce a 'clean' and characterless spirit but to retain certain of the impurities deliberately in order to lend the whisky its bouquet and highly individual flavour. At the stage of selecting and rejecting congenerics, as they are called, the distiller's intuition is superior to all other factors, and in spite of the improvements brought to the industry by modern science the inherited skill of the Highland distillery worker is paramount. Without human excellence there would be no excellent Highland pot-still malt whisky. There would be malt, and grain, and of course a multiplicity of blends. The entire process might even be taken over by a computer. But that subtle mysterious something which cannot be described would be missing.

VI

THE STORY OF GRAIN

UNTIL the second half of the nineteenth century malt whisky
was principally a Scottish drink, made from Scottish ingredients
and consumed by Scotsmen. Customs-duty evaders from the
days of the illicit still had brought it to England, where it sold as
an agreeable novelty, but on the continent of Europe Scotch
whisky was virtually unknown. The rich man's drink was
brandy, and in Scotland, as Burns has told us, whisky was 'the
poor man's wine'—selling at about two-and-sixpence a bottle.
Sir Winston Churchill once wrote: 'My father could never have
drunk whisky except when shooting on a moor or in some very
dull chilly place. He lived in the age of brandy and soda.' But
all this was to change irreversibly with the invention of the
patent-still.

As Neil Gunn describes it in his *Whisky and Scotland*, a

patent-still is 'an affair of two tall columns, heated by steam, into which wash is poured at one end and out of which practically pure alcohol pours at the other.' Who invented the method is not exactly clear, but on its introduction it was taken up by the enterprising Stein family in the Lowlands, already established as exporters of Scotch to England from their distillery at Kilbagie in Clackmannan. Robert Stein patented a still on this principle in 1826 and no doubt took further advantage of the vastly improved version developed by Aeneas Coffey, an Inspector-General of Excise in Dublin, four years later. The coming of the Coffey patent-still made a tremendous difference to the entire concept of Scotch whisky making. It has obvious commercial advantages in that it can produce whisky by a continuous process, more cheaply and in far greater quantities than the orthodox pot-still. It heralded a revolution in the industry.

The patent-still is designed to produce a whisky out of a mixture of malted and unmalted barley mashed with maize and other cereals, but because the malt is not dried over a peat fire there are no peaty undertones and the oils and aromatic substances which give malt whisky its special flavour are missing. Patent-still grain whisky is a light potable spirit which lends itself admirably to mixing with malt whiskies to make the fine blends which today sell increasingly well throughout the whisky-drinking world.

Grain distilleries, because they are freer from the benign tyrannies of soil and air, may be established anywhere. Therefore the main patent-still plants of Scotland are situated in or near big towns with fuel available and road and rail transport easily to hand. One of the most modern of these, both in layout and operation, is that of William Grant & Sons Ltd at Girvan in Ayrshire. It represents the first entry into grain whisky making of the firm who are traditionally pot-still distillers and blenders. Girvan Distillery now provides Grant's with all their supplies of grain whisky for blending and for marketing to other blenders.

What happens, briefly, is this. The fermenting of the worts with yeast is done in much the same way as in the preparation of malt whisky. A succession of hot waters is applied to the grain, formerly one part of malted barley to four parts of cooked maize, and the resultant sugary solution is drawn off and piped into a series of 'wash-backs', each holding 50,000 gallons or more. Yeast is added, and the sugars in solution in the worts are quickly transformed into alcohol. The wash, rich in this alcohol, is then pumped to the Coffey still.

All Coffey stills are similar in principle, the method of continuous production having changed only in application since the invention of the first. To explain their workings, however, without recourse to technicalities, is a formidable task. John Doxat manages it in *Drinks and Drinking*, and so in erudite detail does Anne Glen in Grant's own magazine *Focus*. In my own case, having been shown every stage of the patent-still operation, I would summarise the process as follows.

The patent-still is constructed of copper, and consists of two giant rectangular columns, one an analyser and the other a rectifier. The plant is capable of yielding over 100,000 proof gallons of spirit each week on average. The cold wash is pumped into coils at the top of the rectifier and pre-heated by ascending vapours prior to being openly discharged in the top of the analysing column. Steam is fed into the base of the analyser and heats the falling wash, vaporising the alcohol. The alcohol vapours are then transferred to the base of the rectifier and rise through perforated plates (which are cooled by the descending wash pipes). At a designed take-off point spirit is drawn off and fed into spirit receivers holding 15,000 proof gallons each. The rejected distillate (feints) is re-cycled, joining the heated wash at the top of the analyser. From the stillhouse, a pipe leads to the filling store, where the new spirit is filled into barrels and laid down to mature in nearby warehouses for a minimum of three years.

The Girvan plant was opened in 1964. Besides the big output of grain spirit, it also makes a Lowland malt known as Ladyburn, and both gin and vodka. The rate of production is such that one continuously running still alone provides some 850 proof gallons per hour, there being no interruption other than for cleaning and repair to machinery. Grain spirit can be sold after three years for blending; but gins and vodkas, subject to any special requirements of export markets, are available at once.

VII

THE FINAL PROOF

BEFORE moving on to a gentle concern with how best to use whisky in cooking, it might be useful to explain once and for all what is meant by 'proof'.

When I began writing this book, and let people know what I was up to, I was asked many times if the bold figure on the label of a bottle of Scotch meant, say, 70 per cent pure spirit and 30 per cent water. My reaction was always to look away and shuffle my feet uneasily, for I did not know the answer. Now I do, but in the interests of those who may still be confounded— and I assure you no shame should be attached to this—I shall set down both the official and the shorter version.

The Customs and Excise Act of 1952 defines spirits of proof strength as follows:

Spirits shall be deemed to be at proof if the volume of the ethyl alcohol contained therein made up to the volume of the spirits with distilled water has a weight equal to that of twelve-thirteenths of a volume of distilled water equal to the volume of the spirits, the volume of each liquid being computed as at fifty-one degrees Fahrenheit.

It means that the spirit at 51°F weighs exactly twelve-thirteenths of an equal quantity of distilled water. Spirit strength was once 'proved' when whisky and gunpowder were mixed together and ignited. If the gunpowder flashed it was said to be proved. It was not proved if ignition did not take place. The Clark's hydrometer came into use in the 1740s and continued until a more accurate version by Bartholomew Sikes was adopted in 1818 under the Hydrometer Act. It is still in standard use today.

British, American, and European proof strengths vary. The following are some with their British equivalents:

American	European	British
100	50	87·7
86	43	75
80	40	70

Alcohol from a Coffey still is at about 165° proof, but whisky leaving a pot-still might not be at more than 110° proof. There is always a loss of alcohol in the cask by evaporation, up to 3° of which is condoned by the excise officers; but once bottled, Scotch whisky does not lose its strength and cannot deteriorate in any other way. The loss from all stocks maturing in Scotland, however, is estimated at 17,000,000 proof gallons every year.

This enormous wastage is not due to foolhardy neglect on the part of the distillers; instead it is an essential of the maturation process. Both malt and grain whisky, malt particularly, must be allowed to mature for a minimum of three years before being sold. The receptacles are always oak casks and where possible oak casks that have contained sherry. The latter kind impart a darker shade to the whisky matured in them, which for the sake of uniformity requires that the whisky that is not matured in such casks shall be slightly darkened by the addition of infinitesimal quantities of caramel, except in the case of certain malts, like Glenfiddich and Balvenie, where the golden colour is acquired naturally.

The main reason for using oak wood is that being permeable it allows air to pass in and enough evaporation to take place to remove certain undesirable constituents. Malt whisky, which by reason of its make-up contains more of these, takes longer to mature than grain whisky and is often left in the cask for as long as fifteen years. The congeneric which disperses during maturation is a mild accumulation of fusel oil. Until sixty or so years ago, when maturing was often incomplete, small quantities of this oil might be transferred to the bottle, which is the reason why some people even today turn a new bottle of Scotch upside down before opening. This is now quite superfluous, because distillation and sufficient maturing will have removed the offending precipitates, with the result that the spirit, malt, grain or blended, is of one weight throughout.

It is important to note, too, that when the age of a blended whisky is declared on the label the figure given relates to the youngest and not the oldest spirit in the blend. The label must also affirm the liquid measure of the contents and the strength. The same applies to vatted malts, which come from the mixing of single malt whiskies of different ages and made at different times of the year from the same pot-still distillery.

VIII

COOKING WITH SCOTCH WHISKY

Some men take as readily to cooking as ducks take to drakes. I am not one of them. I know what I like and I invariably eat too much of it, but how comestibles appear on my plate is to me as much a matter for astonishment as it is for delight. I regard the kitchen in my home as a mysterious but necessary gap between the hallway and the garden. I think it is decorated in blue, or perhaps yellow, and every day there comes from under the door a delicious smell of onions or garlic and a sound of cheerful whistling punctuated sometimes by a thud and a cry of rage. Wonderful things happen in this place, but I am content that when dinner-time is here I have only to reach for the salt. Betty, my wife, who is partly Belgian and therefore a brilliant cook, tells me that in her country the salt-cellar is placed on the table purely for decoration, or to oblige the English, for the condiments will already have been added and the dish conscientiously tasted before serving. In the light of such knowledge I now hand over to her.

A. R.-J.

WHEN I was asked if I would be prepared to experiment in cooking with Scotch, my first reaction was one of horror. Possibly this had something to do with my father, a full-bodied Scot who wouldn't even allow ice within a room's-length (*any* room's-length) of *his*. In our house, whisky was almost a religion. Scotch was a man's drink . . . Father's drink . . . the only drink. And if father didn't get through a bottle a day without flinching, then his mind was unnaturally bent upon some less masculine pursuit. Which didn't happen often.

He'd learned to drink whisky, so he said, in Sauchiehall Street, Glasgow, during his years as an apprentice marine engineer, and he wasn't going to stop now. He could certainly take his dram. By evening he had merely mellowed, like a beautiful Balvenie. Drinking whisky, he would inform us, wouldn't kill him. But to stop drinking whisky might. And that was a risk he didn't intend to take.

He was a lovely man, my father. And I suppose now that my reluctance to pop a tot of his favourite brand into the stew was born of a desire not to disturb his soul, wherever it might be. On the other hand, the Scots in me produces not only caution but also a spirit of adventure. And of sensible economy.

Obviously the best whisky to cook with is a pure malt. A 'Glenfiddich' pure malt costs (at the time of going to press) £3·84 and comprises 26⅔ fluid ounces, whereas a three-star, or 'cooking', brandy costs £4 and comprises only 24 fluid ounces. A blended whisky is even cheaper: about £2·70. So I argued with myself and with my father's memory.

Encouraged, I recruited two superlative cooks to help me, Ann Tarlton and Valerie Jackson. Three saucepans were better than one, I felt, in a venture so new and unusual to us all. We didn't, we agreed, need to buy a whole bottle of whisky to start with. And most people, we also agreed, usually had whisky in the house (even if only a blend), whereas very few of us nowadays have even a half-bottle of three-star brandy.

We are now all three completely won over to cooking with Scotch. In our separate kitchens we concocted recipes our husbands and guests thoroughly approved of and for which we received on numerous occasions the final accolade of: 'What did you *put* in it?' (Which, as any woman knows, is quite different from 'Can I have the recipe?')

Eventually I personally became so enthusiastic that I am now popping a tot into everything, just to see if I like it. A tot in the stew come a cold winter's night does no harm to anybody. A tot in the cottage pie, a tot in the Cornish pasty . . . it just depends whether I feel we can afford a tot or not. And by now I wouldn't even think of serving that ubiquitous tomato soup (or any other soup for that matter) without a dollop of cream and a *soupçon* of Scotch to each plate. Scotch is so much more heady than sherry.

Before the reader starts dipping into the following recipes, let me proffer some advice. Firstly, she should realise that the measures of whisky given might not be to the taste of everybody. I think that all alcoholic additives, be they whisky, sherry, brandy or wine, are matters of personal preference. Either you like the bouquet to come over fairly strong or you don't. Try, therefore, some of the easier, cheaper recipes before rushing headlong into Scotched Hare with Pickled Peaches (page 67) or Baba Sobieska (page 72). You will very soon learn to adjust your Scotch to your palate and your purse.

Never, *never* boil the Scotch if you can help it. Bring it *to* the boil, by all means. But then cover it closely or encase it in pastry or mashed potatoes before permitting it to evaporate, leaving your kitchen smelling beautifully boozy but your anxiously-tended dish tasting completely bereft of that little extra something.

Flambé. You will note as you read on that Valerie, Ann, and I were reluctant to *flambé* anything. *Flambé* looks very clever and pretty in front of guests but it vaporises the alcohol immediately and drives off both calories and inebriants. So you can slim and keep sober on *flambé*. But we do feel that it is a frightful waste of whisky. We have been more inclined, therefore, not to set our precious Scotch on fire.

Should you decide to *flambé*, though, use a taper for igniting and don't bend over the dish. Clear the area of inflammable material. And allow the flames to burn down naturally, stirring from time to time with a long-handled spoon (not a *wooden* spoon, either).

Serving numbers. We feel that most cooks take more notice of ingredients than they do of arbitrary serving numbers. A dish might indeed '*Serve four*' if the meal started with, say, Cherington Pâté (page 61) and ended with Highland Oranges and Grapefruit (page 78). By the same token, Pheasant in Whisky Sauce (page 65) could easily '*Serve six*' but, even if there are only two of you, it is still essential to use all the ingredients listed since one cannot buy half a pheasant. On the other hand, it is easy to halve the haunch of venison in Auld Nick's Highland Deer (page 60). We ask our readers, therefore, to assume, as we did, that we were serving *four to six people* and to add or subtract as necessary and according to the appetites and numbers of dishes being offered.

In conclusion, we would all three like to thank the Scotch Whisky Association for a wealth of excellent recipes, the preliminary trying-out of some of which went entirely to our heads and which are all reproduced overleaf.

And, finally, if you haven't got any mace, or cranberries, or shallots, or cayenne, it doesn't matter—really. Just use what you *have* got. After all, blended whisky may not be quite as mellow as pure malt, but it still tastes jolly good once it's in the pot.

B. R.J.

FISH

Kipper toasts

1 packet kipper fillets	6 ounces butter
½ lemon	3 tablespoons whisky

Skin the fillets and leave to soak in the whisky for an hour or so. Melt the butter, squeeze the lemon and blend with the kipper and whisky until completely smooth. Spread on fingers of toast decorated with thin slices of lemon.

Lobster in Speyside sauce

Meat from claws and
    tails of 2 lobsters
3 ounces butter
2 ounces shallots
4 ounces mushrooms
¼ pint whisky
black pepper

6 ounces long-grain rice
1 teaspoon salt
rind and juice of 1 lemon
¼ teaspoon ground cloves
8 ounces skinned tomatoes
¼ pint cream

Slice lobster meat across. Melt 2 ounces butter in casserole and
sauté sliced shallots until soft. Slice and add mushrooms. Stir
in lobster and mix well. Cover and cook very slowly (3 minutes
if lobster is already cooked, 10 minutes if not). Remove lid and
add a little salt, pepper, cloves, quartered tomatoes and cream.
Add the whisky and heat up but do not boil. Shake over a
gentle heat until the whole is well mixed. Cover and keep hot
without boiling for 5 minutes. Place rice in pan and cover with
¾ pint cold water. Add 1 ounce butter, salt and lemon, and
bring to boil. Simmer slowly until all the water has been
absorbed. Cover with a cloth and allow to steam for 5 minutes.
The rice will take 12 minutes to cook and should be stirred with
a fork when the cloth is removed. Turn out the rice and pile the
creamed lobster in the centre.

Loch Leven trout

4 medium brown or rainbow
    trout
1½ ounces butter
2 ounces flaked brown
    almonds

seasoned flour
lemon wedges
3 tablespoons whisky

Toss the whole fish in seasoned flour. Melt the butter in a large
frying pan. When it begins to froth, add the trout. Cook 5
minutes each side, then add almonds and toss lightly until hot.
Pour in the whisky (which can be flamed if you can bear to).

Add a squeeze of lemon juice and serve very hot with lemon wedges.

Prawns and rice

1 pound prawns	½ gill double cream
4 ounces rice	2 teaspoons cornflour
2 ounces butter	4 tablespoons whisky
2 tablespoons olive oil	4 tablespoons white wine
1 small chopped onion	seasoning
2 cloves crushed garlic	cayenne
2 peeled tomatoes	

Cook the rice and keep warm. Melt butter and oil and fry onion and garlic until translucent. Add prawns, chopped tomatoes, season well and sauté. Warm half the whisky in a soup-ladle and add to the mixture. Flame. Pour on the wine and keep at a low heat for a few minutes. Remove the fish and keep warm. Mix together the remaining whisky, cream and cornflour and add to the sauce. Bring to the boil; remove almost immediately from heat and stir, adding cayenne and adjusting the seasoning. Serve the prawns on a bed of rice with the sauce poured over.

Prawns in whisky

A slightly more exotic variety of *Prawns and rice*.

1 pound frozen prawns	freshly-ground black pepper
4 tablespoons butter	cayenne pepper
4 tablespoons olive oil	6 tablespoons whisky
2 tablespoons finely chopped shallots (or onion)	6 tablespoons dry white wine
1 clove garlic, finely chopped	1 teaspoon cornflour
2 tomatoes, peeled, seeded, and chopped	4 tablespoons double cream
	1 pinch dried tarragon
salt	1 egg yolk
	boiled rice

Combine butter and oil in a frying-pan. Add finely chopped shallots (or onion) and garlic and sauté until transparent. Add

prawns, tomatoes, salt, pepper, cayenne to taste. Sauté gently
for a few minutes. Pour over 4 tablespoons whisky and flame.
Add wine and simmer for 5 minutes. Remove prawns and keep
warm. Combine remaining whisky, cornflour and cream, add
to sauce and beat vigorously over a high flame until sauce comes
to the boil. Boil for only 1 minute. Remove from heat. Add
tarragon and pour a little hot sauce over the egg yolk. Mix well
and then stir in the rest of the egg to the sauce. Pour over
prawns and serve immediately with rice.

Lobster à l'écossaise

2 large lobsters	1 teaspoon beef extract
¼ cup olive oil	bouquet garni
4 small onions	2 tablespoons butter
1 clove garlic	juice of ½ lemon
½ cup dry white wine	salt
¼ cup whisky	black pepper
2 tablespoons tomato paste	cayenne

Cut lobsters into 3–4 pieces and add all other eatable meat.
Heat oil in large pan and add lobster. Sprinkle with salt and
pepper and cook gently for 5 minutes. Meanwhile fry finely
chopped onion and garlic in 1 tablespoon butter until transparent. Add to the lobster with the white wine. You can now
also add the whisky and *flambé* if you want to, but I prefer to
put it in later (which is not strictly conventional; however, at
the price lobsters are these days, possibly anybody making this
dish doesn't feel too badly about also lighting the whisky!). Heat
up a little and then add tomato paste, beef extract, and bouquet
garni and cook 10 minutes over a moderate flame. Put the
lobster meat on a deep, heated dish. Add 1 tablespoon butter,
lemon juice, a dash of cayenne and the whisky if not previously
flamed, and bring to the boil. Immediately pour this over the
lobster. It smells just as delicious as it tastes.

St Cyrus crab scallops

Sauce
½ small onion
1 clove
½ pint milk
bay leaf
1 ounce butter
1 ounce flour
salt and pepper

Scallops
6 ounces tinned crab
1 ounce butter
dry breadcrumbs
4 ounces mushrooms
salt, pepper and cayenne
2 tablespoons whisky

Stick the clove in the onion and warm gently in a pan with the milk and bay leaf. Allow to infuse for 30 minutes. Melt the butter and cook with the flour, then strain in the milk, stirring all the time. Return to the heat and, stirring constantly, allow to boil for 3 minutes. Season to taste. Sauté the peeled and sliced mushrooms in the ounce of butter, then stir in mushrooms, flaked crab, whisky, and cayenne to taste. Mix thoroughly, without boiling. Divide between 4–6 scallop shells, sprinkle with crumbs, dot with butter and re-heat for 6 minutes at Gas 7/425°F and serve immediately.

Turbot Kinloch

4 turbot steaks
fish stock
2 ounces butter
¾ pound tomatoes
parsley
1 minced onion

4 ounces peeled fresh prawns
3 tablespoons whisky
seasoning
mace, lemon juice,
   peppercorns
pinch of sugar

Poach fish steaks gently for 5–6 minutes in water to cover, flavoured with mace, lemon juice and peppercorns. Melt butter and gently sauté minced onion. Add chopped tomatoes, simmer for 10 minutes, then add salt, pepper, ¼ pint of stock and a pinch of sugar. Do not allow the liquid to dry out. Add whisky and prawns and simmer very gently for 5 minutes. Put the poached fish on a deep warm dish and spoon the liquid over. Garnish with chopped parsley.

Whisky dip

1 teacup cooked shrimp (chopped)	3 teaspoons minced chives
1 teacup sour cream	4 teaspoons minced parsley
$\frac{1}{4}$ teacup whisky	$\frac{1}{2}$ teaspoon salt
1 teaspoon dill (minced or dried)	$\frac{1}{2}$ teaspoon cayenne
	$\frac{1}{4}$ teaspoon pepper

Blend all ingredients until smooth, chill, and serve with 'dips' such as potato crisps (unflavoured), chunks of French bread, sticks of celery, or cheese biscuits. Increase amounts according to number of guests. This amount can easily be absorbed by 4 people.

Whisky fish Jackson

1 large packet of frozen plaice fillets	knob of butter
	1 teaspoon chopped chives
1 sliced shallot or a small onion	$2\frac{1}{2}$ tablespoons whisky

Fry shallot or onion in butter until soft. Season the fish and roll it up. Add the fish and 2 tablespoons whisky to the pan, cover and cook over a low flame for about 15 minutes. Add chives, re-cover and cook for a further 5 minutes. Add a further $\frac{1}{2}$ tablespoon of whisky, and reheat before serving.

MEAT AND POULTRY

Angus casserole

2 pounds best stewing steak	2 onions
2 tablespoons beef dripping	1 pound carrots
2 crushed garlic cloves	1 tin tomatoes
5 tablespoons whisky	1 pint stock *or* $\frac{1}{2}$ stock, $\frac{1}{2}$ red
salt, black pepper	wine

Marinate steak in whisky for 24 hours before cooking. Reserve juices when marinated. Set oven at Gas 5/375°F. Melt dripping and fry cubed steak, dusted with seasoned flour, until just brown. Remove from pan. Add to pan chopped onion, carrots and crushed garlic. Stir occasionally until onions begin to brown. Put meat into casserole dish and spoon tomatoes and rest of vegetables over it. Add the marinating juice and the pint of stock/red wine. Season to taste and cover closely. Cook for 2 hours.

Auld Nick's Highland deer

4 pounds haunch of venison
½ gill cooking oil
9 tablespoonfuls whisky
juice of 1 lemon
1 sliced onion

Sauce
2 ounces margarine
2 onions

1 small tin tomatoes
2 sticks celery
9 tablespoons whisky
1 tablespoon Worcester sauce
½ pint dry ginger ale
1 ounce brown sugar
1 bay leaf
2 teaspoons cornflour

Tie venison securely. Blend oil, whisky, lemon and seasoning and place in a deep plate or tin. Add sliced onion and lay venison in this marinade, spooning the liquor over and turning the meat from time to time. Leave for up to 24 hours. Transfer venison to tightly-covered roasting tin and pour over marinade. Roast at Gas 5/375°F for 2½ hours until tender.

Sauce: Melt margarine and fry onions until soft. Stir in the rest of the ingredients except cornflour, which should be blended with 1 tablespoon water. Simmer sauce for 40 minutes, then add cornflour and simmer 3 minutes. Serve with redcurrant jelly, creamed potatoes and a green vegetable.

Cherington pâté

Ann Tarlton explains how her 'rough old pâté' (which is delicious) came into being: 'I discovered it quite by accident one day when there was a pheasant merrily roasting in my oven which, when I remembered it, was a bit dry to say the least. I caught sight of the whisky bottle and thought a touch of "marinating" wouldn't harm the bird . . .'

1 pheasant or chicken (cooked)	salt
	black pepper
½ pound lamb's or calf's liver	parsley, rosemary and thyme
¼ pound mushrooms	orange slices for decoration
clove of garlic	bay leaves for decoration
2 eggs	4–5 rashers of bacon
2 tablespoons orange juice	clarified butter
4 tablespoons whisky	

Line pâté dish with bacon. Fry chopped garlic, chopped liver and mushrooms. Allow to cool. Mince together pheasant (or chicken), liver, mushrooms, garlic, parsley, rosemary and thyme. Mix in eggs, orange juice and whisky. Add seasoning. Put into pâté dish and cover with bacon and bay leaves. Stand dish in a pan of water and cook in oven at Gas 3/325°F for 1½ hours. Allow to cool. When pâté is quite cold, decorate with orange slices and pour over clarified butter. Chill.

Chicken and scampi cardean

3½ pounds chicken	2 tablespoons flour
2 sticks celery	Worcester sauce
1 onion	3 tablespoons whisky
10 ounces rice	2 ounces butter
8 ounces scampi (cooked)	

Put the chicken in a deep casserole with 1 pint water, celery and seasoning. Cook in oven at Gas 5/350°F for 1½ hours. Strain the stock and remove flesh from bones. Boil rice for 12 minutes in stock and more water if necessary. Drain well. Sauté the minced onion in the butter until just browning and add the rice. Cook until browned and keep warm. Mix the flour with a few drops Worcester sauce and add a little cold water. Mix with 1 pint chicken stock and season to taste. Add the whisky. Put the chicken, scampi and sauce in the casserole, cover closely, and reheat for 20 minutes at Gas 5/375°F. Dish up with rice in the middle, surrounded by chicken and scampi.

Faskelly veal chops

4 veal chops	1 ounce butter
2 ounces mushrooms	½ gill chicken stock
1 teaspoon tomato purée	chopped parsley
1 minced onion	2 tablespoons whisky

Melt the butter in a frying-pan and brown the veal on both sides for 2–3 minutes. Add the minced onion and continue cooking over a moderate heat until the onion is brown. Add the mushrooms and cook gently for 5 minutes. Add the whisky (and flame it if you must . . . but I don't). Mix the purée into the stock and pour it into the pan and season. Cover closely and allow to cook gently for about 10 minutes. Sprinkle with chopped parsley before serving.

Ham mousse

8 ounces cooked ham	4 ounces skinned, chopped
4 ounces cooked tongue	tomatoes
1½ ounces butter	1 teaspoon anchovy essence
4 ounces mushrooms	¼ pint cream
5 tablespoons whisky	2 whites of eggs
½ ounce flour	½ ounce gelatine
¼ pint milk	½ gill water
1 teaspoon French mustard	2-pint mould

Mince ham and tongue. Melt 1 ounce butter and fry mushrooms slowly for 3 minutes. Pour whisky over (and ignite if you wish). When the flames have died down, mix with ham mixture. Melt remaining butter, stir in flour and add milk. Whisk until smooth and add to ham. Stir in mustard, tomatoes and essence. Whip cream lightly and egg whites stiffly. Dissolve gelatine in water and stir into mixture, fold in cream and whites. Stir lightly until it begins to set and then turn quickly into an oiled mould. Chill. Turn on to a chilled serving dish. Garnish with green salad and home-made mayonnaise.

Highland chicken

4 chicken quarters	¼ pint single cream
4 tablespoons butter	3 tablespoons whisky
juice of ½ lemon	seasoning
1 tablespoon French mustard	

Beat 3 tablespoons softened butter, mustard, lemon juice, and seasoning into a paste with 3 tablespoons whisky and spread over the chicken. Melt 1 tablespoon butter in a casserole and brown the chicken all over. Cover and cook gently for 30 minutes. Pour the rest of the whisky over the chicken, warm it, and flame it. Pour in the cream and cook without boiling for 10 minutes.

Highland pheasant

1 pheasant	thyme
8 ounces raisins	5 tablespoons whisky
¼ pint single cream	chopped onion
parsley	

Joint pheasant and cook in hot butter to brown. Add warm whisky and ignite. Add chopped onion, parsley, herbs and seasoning. Cover tightly and cook slowly for 15 minutes. Add washed and dried raisins and cook for a further 45 minutes. Just before serving, stir in cream, but do not boil once cream is added.

Kidneys Crighton

12 lamb's kidneys (halved, skinned and cored)
1 ounce flour
1 ounce butter
large onion (peeled and finely sliced)

¼ teaspoon mace
3 tablespoons single cream
⅓ pint whisky and dry white wine mixed
seasoning

Toss kidneys in seasoned flour and fry in butter for 2–3 minutes to seal. Keep in warm place. Add onion to pan, fry until soft but not coloured. Stir in any excess flour with mace and whisky and wine mixture. Loosen sediment and just bring to boiling point. Remove from heat and stir in cream. Adjust seasoning and pour over kidneys. Cover closely and cook in oven for about 30 minutes at Gas 3/325°F.

Ladywell pie

1 rabbit
¾ pound puff pastry
¾ pound salt belly of pork

Sauce
1 large onion
½ pint brown stock
1 tablespoon flour
6 tablespoons whisky

Forcemeat
rabbit liver
2 ounces breadcrumbs
lemon thyme
seasoning
2 ounces fat bacon
parsley
nutmeg
egg to bind

Soak the rabbit joints in cold water for 1 hour. Mince the liver and the bacon and add the rest of the forcemeat ingredients. Form small balls with the mixture. Dice the salt pork and cook in a heavy pan until the fat runs and the meat is crisp. Remove the meat, and place in a pie dish with the rabbit and forcemeat balls. Brown the onion in some of the pork fat and add flour

LOBSTER IN SPEYSIDE SAUCE

AULD NICK'S HIGHLAND DEER

CHERINGTON PÂTÉ

PHEASANT IN WHISKY SAUCE

SCOTCH CHICKEN

GLENFIDDICH WHISKY'D ORANGES

BLACK BUN

A DAISY, A ZOOM AND A SCOTCH TOM COLLINS

and stock. Cook until thick. Season to taste and add the whisky. Pour over meat in pie dish. Put on the puff pastry top and brush with any remaining egg. Bake in a moderate oven, Gas 6/400°F, for 1–1½ hours.

Pheasant Normande

1 plump pheasant	2 Cox's apples
1 ounce clarified butter	¼ pint jellied stock
2 shallots	bouquet garni
8 tablespoons whisky	¼ pint double cream
flour or slaked arrowroot	

Brown the pheasant on all sides in the butter. Add the finely chopped shallots to the pan and cook until golden. Flame with 4 tablespoons whisky and reduce by half. Tip on the stock, add the peeled, cored and sliced apples, seasonings, bouquet garni, and the rest of the whisky and bring to the boil. Cover tightly and cook gently for about 50 minutes. Take out the pheasant, carve, and arrange in a hot serving dish. Pass the contents of the casserole through a fine sieve or nylon strainer and return to the rinsed pan. Thicken lightly with flour or very little slaked arrowroot. Heat the cream, add to the sauce, adjust the seasoning, and spoon over the pheasant.

Pheasant in whisky sauce

1 pheasant	*Sauce*
1 potato	¼ pint whisky
2 ounces butter	2 ounces butter
8 tablespoons whisky	2 ounces flour
rind of 1 large orange	2 onions
8 ounces cranberries	1 carrot
seasoning	4 ounces mushrooms
	juice of 1 orange
	1 tablespoon bramble jelly

Clean and truss the pheasant and place the peeled potato inside the bird to prevent moisture during cooking. Place in a roasting-tin. Spread butter and orange rind over the breast and pour on the 8 tablespoons whisky. Dust with pepper. Roast in the centre of the oven at Gas 5/375°F in a covered tin for 45 minutes, basting once or twice. Remove from tin and joint. Strain juices and keep.

Sauce: Melt butter, add sliced onions and sauté without browning for 5 minutes. Add grated carrot and sliced mushrooms and fry 3 minutes. Mix in the flour and stir over a steady heat until pale gold. Add 1 pint water to which has been added the strained gravy from the roasting. Boil and then stir in the whisky, orange juice and bramble jelly. Season to taste and pour over the pheasant joints in a large casserole. Place in centre of oven covered with lid or foil and cook another 45 minutes. Remove lid and spread cranberries on top. Press them lightly into the sauce and return the dish to the oven for 10 minutes. Garnish with cranberries.

Scotch chicken

1½ pounds chicken or *poussin*
2 ounces butter
4 tablespoons whisky
¼ pint single cream
seasoning

(Double these ingredients for 4 people. But cook each chicken separately.)

Cut the chicken in two and cook it in melted butter for about 20 minutes. Add seasoning to taste. When cooked, remove chicken and keep it warm. Keep a little of the fat, add the whisky and run it around the pan. Add the cream and warm, but do not boil. Pour over chicken before serving.

Scotched hare with pickled peaches

1 small jointed hare
1 ounce flour
1 teaspoon paprika
1 teaspoon salt
2 ounces butter
2 ounces streaky bacon
2 small onions
2 sticks chopped celery
¼ teaspoon dried or chopped thyme
¼ teaspoon dried or chopped mint

½ teaspoon ground cloves
2 teaspoons Worcester sauce
12 tablespoons whisky
¾ pint stock
1 tin peach halves
2 ounces demerara sugar
1 gill peach juice
2 teaspoons tarragon vinegar
¼ teaspoon ground ginger
¼ teaspoon ground cinnamon

Select leg and back joints which are well covered with meat. Place others in pan and cover with a pint of water. Simmer for 30 minutes. Strain and use this as the stock. Mix flour with salt and paprika. Toss chosen joints in this until well covered. Melt butter and fry bacon. Then fry floured hare joints in this until well browned. Lay them in a large casserole. Fry onions until brown, add celery, herbs and spices and fry lightly. Stir in juices, stock and 9 tablespoons whisky and just bring to the boil. Pour over hare and cover tightly. Place in oven one-third down from the top at Gas 5/375°F for 2 hours until tender. A longer time in the oven will merely improve the flavour.

Drain the peach halves. Place sugar and juice in a pan with spices and simmer 3 minutes. Add vinegar and rest of the whisky and pour over peaches. Leave to stand while casserole is cooking. Serve in a deep dish with the liquid poured over and accompanied with baked potatoes.

Tipsy chicken livers

1 pound chicken livers
chopped onion
2 ounces butter
vegetable oil
4 ounces mushrooms
1 dessertspoon tubed tomato
  purée

2 skinned and chopped
  tomatoes
$\frac{3}{8}$ pint chicken stock
4 tablespoons whisky
rice as required
parsley

Wash the livers and halve them. Simmer the chopped onion in butter and oil in a large frying-pan until it is translucent. Add the livers and toss them about to cook evenly. Sprinkle with salt and pepper. While the livers are still pink inside, lift them on to a hot dish and keep them warm. Quickly cook the mushrooms, thickly sliced, in the same pan and add them to the livers. To the residue in the pan add tomatoes, purée, stock and whisky. Heat up without boiling, taste and season further if necessary. Add chicken livers and mushrooms, heat through, and pile in the middle of a border of rice. Decorate with chopped parsley.

Tongue Caledonia

$\frac{3}{4}$ pound sliced tongue
1 large onion
2 ounces butter
1 tin jellied consommé
$\frac{1}{4}$ pint tinned tomatoes
chopped parsley

2 tablespoons raisins
2 ounces flour
$\frac{1}{2}$ teaspoon French mustard
seasoning
2 tablespoons whisky

Soak the raisins in whisky for 2 hours. Sauté the chopped onion in butter and add the flour. Brown well. Make the consommé up to $\frac{3}{4}$ pint with water and add it to the flour with the tomatoes, mustard and seasonings. Boil for 5 minutes, stirring. Put a little sauce on the bottom of an ovenproof dish and lay the meat on top of it. Mix the raisins and whisky with the rest of the sauce, heat and pour over the meat. Place covered in a moderate oven, Gas 6/400°F, for 7–8 minutes until hot.

Spare ribs and barbecue sauce

Allow ¾ pound of spare
  ribs per person.
Crush a clove of garlic and
  add:
1 ¼-teacup made mustard

1 ¼-teacup soy sauce
1 ¼-teacup whisky
1 ¼-teacup demerara sugar
1 dessertspoon grated orange
  rind

Combine ingredients, spread over the ribs, and marinate for a few hours, or overnight, keeping the dish covered. Roast, covered, in medium oven for 1½–2 hours, turning and basting during cooking.

Veal McKay

This delicious recipe was given to us by 'Bice' McKay, who passed the full Cordon Bleu course in Paris before the war and is the very best cook I have ever known.

4 veal chops
  (pork chops may be used,
  but all the fat must be
  removed)

4 dessertspoons whisky
7 ounces grated cheese
1 egg
¼ pint single cream

Mix the cheese, egg and cream together in a bowl. Gently fry chops both sides in a casserole with a lid but do not brown. Divide the cheese mixture into 4, and spread on to each chop. Add a dessertspoon of whisky to each chop, put the lid on the pan and let the chops cook very slowly for about 30 minutes.

Whisky pâté

(With, according to Valerie Jackson, 'as much whisky as you feel you can spare'.)

1 pound chicken livers
6 ounces butter
1 chopped onion
1 dessertspoon chopped parsley

thyme to taste
clove of crushed garlic
seasoning
2 slices chopped bacon

Chop up the onion and fry it in 2 ounces butter until it is soft. Add the livers, crushed garlic, parsley, thyme, salt, pepper and chopped bacon and fry lightly until the liver is just cooked through. Mince or blend this mixture. Add whisky and the melted remaining 4 ounces butter. Pack into a pâté dish and chill.

Whisky wieners

4 veal fillets
2 ounces butter
¼ pint whisky
½ pint thick white sauce
1 small tin tomato purée
1 bay leaf
thyme

1 chopped celery stick
1 chopped small onion
sliced stuffed green olives
seasoning
anchovy fillets
beaten egg and breadcrumbs

Dip the fillets in egg and breadcrumbs. Melt the butter and fry the veal slowly until golden. Make a white sauce and add tomato purée, bay leaf, thyme, celery, onion and seasoning. Cook for several minutes, remove the bay leaf and add the whisky. Whisk hard while reheating. Arrange veal on a hot dish, pour sauce over, decorate with olives and anchovies and serve at once. This dish tastes very strongly of alcohol! Beginners might be advised to try only half the whisky additive to start with!

SWEETS

Apricot mousse

1 large tin apricots

4 eggs

½ ounce granulated sugar

¼ pint apricot purée

¼ pint double cream

9 tablespoons whisky

¼ ounce gelatine

2 tablespoons water

Drain apricots and set aside about 6 halves. Sieve or liquidise the rest and make up to ¼ pint with apricot juice. Separate eggs and whisk 4 yolks, sugar and apricot purée over hot water until thick. Continue to whisk until cool. Whip cream until light but not buttery, and 2 egg whites until stiff. Dissolve gelatine in water and add to purée mixture. Fold in cream and egg whites until smooth. Grease a 1½ pint mould and cover the top with greaseproof paper. Spread apricot halves on paper and pour the whisky over them. Spoon mousse in on top and chill until set. Loosen from sides and invert in a glass dish. Serve with double cream flavoured with a little whisky.

Atholl brose

Most people think of this as a drink. Val Jackson describes her version, below, as 'the most beautiful pudding ever invented'. You will find the drink recipe, which is quite different, on page 94.

1 pint double cream

4 dessertspoonfuls clear honey

4 nips of whisky

Half-whip the cream. Blend honey and whisky in a bowl until liquid. Pour slowly into cream, whipping the mixture until firm. Chill in separate goblets.

Auld Alliance cream

8 ounces prunes
9 tablespoons whisky
grated rind and juice of ½
   lemon
¼ teaspoon ground ginger
1 ounce granulated sugar

1 packet lemon jelly
1-inch cinnamon stick
4 cloves
double cream and flaked
   brown almonds to decorate

Wash prunes and soak in whisky and ½ pint cold water for 48 hours. Then they will require no cooking. Stone and liquidise until smooth. Add lemon rind and juice, ginger and sugar. Dissolve jelly in ½ pint hot water and infuse with cinnamon and cloves until cool. Strain over prune purée and leave until just beginning to set. Spoon into glasses and decorate with cream and flaked brown almonds.

Baba Sobieska

Yeast cake
4 ounces flour
1 teaspoon granulated sugar
1 rounded teaspoon dried
   yeast
½ ounce caster sugar
2 eggs
2 ounces butter

Filling
½ pint double cream
1 ounce granulated sugar
2 tablespoons whisky
½ teaspoon lemon rind

Fruit
1 small tin apricots
1 small tin tangerines
1 small tin cherries

Syrup
4 ounces brown sugar
½ ounce root ginger
4 cloves
1-inch cinnamon stick
1½ gills mixed fruit juices
9 tablespoons whisky

Sift flour. Mix granulated sugar with ½ gill hot water and sprinkle yeast on surface. Stir and leave until frothy. Add caster sugar to flour and mix with yeast. Beat eggs and add by degrees with

small pats of the butter. Beat well to form a rich batter. Grease
an 8-inch baba tin and fill two-thirds with mixture. Leave in
a warm place until it has risen to the top of the tin, which will
take about 35–45 minutes. Bake in the centre of oven at Gas 6/
400°F until well risen, richly browned and shrinking from the
sides of the tin (about 25–35 minutes). Loosen and invert on to
serving dish.

Now make up the syrup by heating the sugar in the fruit juices
from the tins and adding the spices. Cover and leave to infuse
for 10 minutes. Reheat if necessary, add the whisky, and strain
over the baba. Beat cream until stiff and stir in sugar and whisky
with lemon rind. Stone cherries and use to decorate. Fill the
centre of the baba with alternate layers of fruit and cream,
finishing with a thick layer of cream.

Baked bananas flambés

8 not-too-ripe bananas	$\frac{1}{2}$ lemon
5 ounces butter	8 tablespoons whisky

Peel bananas and split lengthwise. Then melt the butter in a
shallow baking dish and arrange the bananas in it, round side
uppermost. Sprinkle each banana-half lightly with brown sugar
and place in oven at Gas 8/450°F. After 10 minutes squeeze the
lemon juice over the bananas. Baste and replace in the oven for
another 3–4 minutes. Meanwhile slightly warm the whisky.
Baste the bananas once more, bring the dish immediately to the
table, pour the whisky over them and blaze.

Glenfiddich whisky'd oranges

9 oranges	9 tablespoons water
6 tablespoons demerara sugar	9 tablespoons whisky

Peel and thinly slice the oranges, removing all pips and pith. (A
serrated-edge knife is ideal for this.) Save the juice on the plate.

Put sugar, whisky, water and orange juice in a shallow frying-pan. Melt the sugar over a low heat and simmer for 2 minutes. Add the orange slices and turn up the heat for 1–2 minutes. Remove from heat and arrange in a dish, pour over the juice from pan and chill. Serve with cream or ice-cream.

Crêpes Mary Stuart

4 ounces plain flour	*Syrup*
2 eggs	1 ounce lump sugar
1 ounce butter	1 small orange
1½ gills creamy milk	½ lemon
cooking oil	¼ pint whisky
	2 ounces butter

Sift flour. Beat 2 egg yolks and 1 egg white together and stir carefully into flour with melted butter and half the milk. Beat until smooth and then add rest of milk. Oil a small omelette pan and heat gently. Pour batter into a jug. Tip enough batter into the pan to cover the base thickly. Fry lightly and then turn over and fry on the other side. Fold in half and keep warm. Continue until all batter has been used, piling the crêpes on top of one another as they are made.

Wash orange and lemon skins. Rub the sugar lumps over the fruit to remove the zest. Squeeze out juices and place sugar, juices, whisky and the 2 ounces butter in the omelette pan. Heat but do not boil. Lift each crêpe into this syrup once the sugar has melted, and coat on each side. Fold each into four. Serve overlapping in a dish and *flambé* with a further tot of whisky if desired—though it isn't strictly necessary.

Edinburgh vacherin

Meringue
3 egg whites
3 ounces caster sugar
4 ounces icing sugar
1 teaspoon vanilla essence
3 7-inch rounds of rice paper

To decorate
chopped pistachio nuts

Filling
4 ounces butter
4 ounces icing sugar
6 tablespoons whisky
3 ounces chopped walnuts
1½ ounces grated milk
  chocolate
2 ounces peppermint creams

Whisk egg whites with sugars and vanilla essence over hot water or in an electric mixer until stiff. Continue to whisk until cool. Pipe or spread on to three rounds of rice paper and decorate one with chopped nuts. Bake at Gas ½/200°F until firm, which can take 2–3 hours. Beat butter and sieved icing sugar until white. Beat in egg yolks and whisky. Add chopped walnuts and finely grated milk chocolate. Break peppermint creams into small pieces and stir in. Use to sandwich the three vacherins together. Chill and serve with ice-cream.

Flora's whisky omelette

6 eggs
½ ounce butter
1 tablespoon granulated sugar

2 tablespoons whisky
1 tablespoon Curaçao or
  Cointreau liqueur

Separate egg yolks and whisk whites until stiff enough to stand in peaks. Beat the yolks and then fold into whites. Melt butter in a frying-pan until just about to turn brown. Spread mixture evenly over the bottom of the pan and cook over a medium heat until the underside is just brown. Loosen the edges and then place under a medium grill for 2–3 minutes to brown lightly and set the top. Take immediately to the table, sprinkle with the sugar, pour over the whisky and liqueur mixture, and flame.

Fluffy banana Balmoral

6 bananas	3 dessertspoons caster sugar
3 eggs	1 tablespoon whisky
pinch of salt	

Mash the bananas. Separate the eggs and beat the yolks with the sugar until thick. Fold in the fruit and whisky. Stiffly whip the whites with a pinch of salt. Fold into the mixture. Chill for at least 20 minutes and serve with *langues de chats* or boudoir biscuits.

Gaelic coffee mousse

6 eggs	½ pint double cream
3 tablespoons instant coffee	4 tablespoons golden syrup
2 tablespoons boiling water	1 ounce gelatine
6 ounces sugar	6 tablespoons whisky

Dissolve the instant coffee in the boiling water and melt the gelatine in 8 tablespoons water. Separate the eggs and whisk the yolks, syrup, 4 ounces of the sugar and coffee over hot water until thick and creamy. Remove from heat and whisk until cool. Add the gelatine and whisky and fold them in. Beat the egg whites until stiff with a pinch of salt and the rest of the sugar. Fold into mixture. Lightly whip the cream and fold it in quickly. Allow to set in a mould or dish.

Gaelic cream

4 eggs	½ pint double cream
2 ounces caster sugar	2 fluid ounces whisky

Separate eggs and beat yolks and sugar together over hot water. Then allow to cook slowly, stirring all the time, on top of a double boiler until hot and frothy. Remove from heat. Stir in whisky and allow to cool. Whisk egg whites until stiff and whip

the cream. Turn into a 3-pint mould and leave to set. This dish
is best made the day before it is to be served.

Glenfiddich syllabub

1 small glass (4 fluid ounces) white wine or sherry	2 ounces sugar
2 tablespoons whisky	½ pint double cream
1 lemon	nutmeg

Soak lemon rind in white wine, lemon juice, and whisky overnight. Strain liquid and gradually add the sugar. Whip the
cream with the mixture until it stands in peaks. Serve in tall
glasses, dusted with nutmeg, and with a macaroon as accompaniment.

Gordon's mincemeat tart

1 pound sweet shortcrust pastry	1 egg yolk
1 ounce butter	½ ounce plain flour
4 ounces currants	2 tablespoons whisky
4 ounces chopped, candied peel	2 ounces soft brown sugar
2 ounces chopped walnuts	cinnamon or allspice to taste double cream

Line a flan dish with pastry and bake blind. Melt butter in
saucepan and add flour, cooking until thick. Beat egg yolk. Add
currants, chopped nuts, peel, egg yolk, whisky and sugar to the
butter and flour. Add cinnamon or allspice to taste. Cook in
oven at Gas 4/350°F for 30 minutes. Serve either hot or cold
with cream.

Grant's chocolate pudding

Ann Tarlton's recipe, to which she has added the comment 'N.B. Very Rich'.

4 ounces plain chocolate
1 tablespoon single cream
2 ounces crushed digestive
   biscuit crumbs

2 ounces butter
3 tablespoons whisky
2 teaspoons brown sugar

Melt chocolate in bowl over hot water. Remove from heat and beat in butter. Stir in remaining ingredients. Pour into glass bowl and chill until ready to eat.

Highland oranges and grapefruit

5 oranges
2 grapefruit
double cream (optional)

4 tablespoons whisky
sugar to taste

Peel and cut fruit into thin slices. Layer with sugar in a glass bowl. Pour the whisky over. Cover and chill for several hours. Can be served with or without double cream.

Iced coffee soufflé

4 eggs
4 ounces granulated sugar
4 tablespoons powdered coffee
2 ounces plain chocolate

2 tablespoons whisky
½ pint double cream
grated chocolate for
   decoration

Separate eggs and beat yolks with sugar and powdered coffee until mixture is thick and creamy. Melt chocolate with 2 tablespoons water in a small saucepan. Add whisky and stir into egg and coffee mixture. Whisk egg whites and whip cream and fold into mixture. Pour into individual dishes and freeze for 4 hours. Decorate with grated chocolate.

Christmas peaches

large tin of peaches   9 dessertspoons mincemeat
4 tablespoons whisky

Drain peaches and add 2 tablespoons whisky to about three-quarters of the juice. Arrange peaches, inside-up, in a dish. Divide the mincemeat up among the centres and then add a teaspoon of whisky to each. Just before serving, heat up the syrup and whisky mixture *without boiling* and pour over the fruit.

Perthshire peaches

4 fresh peaches   juice of 2 oranges
2 tablespoons honey   3 tablespoons whisky
toasted chopped almonds

Peel peaches, halve and remove stone. Arrange on long shallow dish, cut side down. Combine honey and orange juice in saucepan and heat gently until honey melts. Add whisky and pour over peaches. Cover and chill. Just before serving, sprinkle with toasted almonds.

Pineapple and ginger torte

Ginger snap paste   ½ gill pineapple juice
4 ounces ginger snaps   ½ gill whisky
2 ounces butter   2 ounces stem ginger
1 tablespoon whisky   2 eggs
                               4 ounces granulated sugar
Filling   1 ounce cornflour
1 teacup chopped pineapple
   (tinned)

Roll ginger snaps until finely crumbed. Melt butter and stir in whisky. Pour onto crumbs and mix together. Press into a deep plate and place in the refrigerator. Place cornflour in a small pan and add pineapple juice. When smooth, add whisky and stir over a gentle heat until thick. Beat in sugar and chopped stem ginger. Separate eggs and beat in each yolk singly. Whisk whites stiffly and fold into mixture with chopped pineapple. Spoon into chilled mixture when set and replace in refrigerator. Serve with cream.

Prince Charlie's soufflé

1 ounce butter	2 tablespoons malt whisky
1 ounce flour	4 eggs
¼ pint milk	15½ ounces tinned raspberries
1 ounce caster sugar	

Melt butter in a pan and then blend in the flour. Cook for a minute. Remove from heat and gradually beat in milk. Add sugar and cook until mixture leaves sides of the pan. Leave to cool and then add the malt whisky. Separate eggs and beat in 3 yolks, one at a time. Whisk 4 egg whites stiffly, and fold in. Pour into a greased soufflé dish and bake in centre of a fairly hot oven, Gas 5/375°F for 35 minutes until golden. Serve at once with raspberries.

Prunes in whisky jelly

1 pound prunes	½ ounce gelatine
3 ounces sugar	7 tablespoons whisky
½ pint double cream	

Soak prunes in water overnight. Add the resulting liquid, made up with water to ¾ pint, to the sugar and boil. Simmer for 3–4 before adding the fruit and then stew gently until cooked. Soak the gelatine in ½ gill cold water and dissolve over a gentle heat. Add to the hot juice. Make up to ¾ pint again with water if necessary. Stone the prunes and chop the flesh. Add the fruit and the whisky to the gelatine and mix while warm. Allow to set in a ring mould. Turn out and fill the centre with whipped, sweetened cream. Pipe stars of cream around the base.

Scotch pineapple

1 fresh pineapple	1 small bottle cocktail cherries
4 ounces demerara sugar	2 ounces sliced browned
6 cloves	almonds
1 inch cinnamon stick	1 large block strawberry
1 inch root ginger	ice-cream
6 tablespoons whisky	$\frac{1}{4}$ pint cream
	1 ounce caster sugar

Cut top from pineapple. Use a small cutter to remove centre core and a small sharp knife to cut off spiky skin from slices $\frac{3}{4}$ inch thick. Dissolve sugar in $\frac{1}{2}$ pint water and add whole spices. Simmer 5 minutes and then remove spices. Add pineapple and simmer a further 5 minutes. Stir in 5 tablespoons whisky and leave to cool. Stone the cherries and add the syrup to the pine-apple. Slice ice-cream into 6 pieces and lay in a large flat dish. Top with pineapple and pour syrup over. Decorate with cherries and top with cream well whipped and flavoured with a little sugar and one tablespoon whisky.

Skye delight

1 teaspoon gelatine	7 tablespoons whisky
1$\frac{1}{2}$ gills milk	1 ounce granulated sugar
2 ounces bitter chocolate	6 tinned peach halves
$\frac{1}{4}$ pint double cream	$\frac{1}{2}$ gill peach juice
2 ounces flaked browned	1 ounce flaked chocolate
almonds	

Place gelatine in pan and add milk. Stir over gentle heat until steaming. Break chocolate into small pieces and add to the pan. Stir until dissolved, but do not boil. Chill until just setting. Whip cream until double its bulk and fold in with 5 tablespoons whisky, almonds and sugar. Place in refrigerator freezing compartment turned to lowest setting. Leave until firm. Turn into basin and beat with wooden spoon until smooth. Replace in freezing tray set at normal. Lay peach halves in a glass dish and cover with the juice mixed with 2 tablespoons whisky. Spoon ice-cream over and dust with flaked chocolate.

Soufflé au Balvenie

2 tablespoons butter	½ teaspoon vanilla essence
2 tablespoons flour	2 tablespoons whisky
½ pint hot milk	halved sponge fingers
pinch salt	(optional)
6 eggs	2 tablespoons cognac
4 tablespoons granulated sugar	(optional)

Melt butter in the top of a double saucepan, add flour and cook, stirring until well blended. Add hot milk and salt. Cook, stirring constantly until smooth and thick and continuing for a few minutes. Let sauce cool slightly. Beat 5 egg yolks with sugar and vanilla essence and mix well with sauce. Stir in whisky. Pre-heat oven to Gas 4/350°F. Line a buttered soufflé dish with halved sponge fingers sprinkled with cognac. Beat 6 egg whites until stiff, but not dry, and fold into cooled mixture. Pour into prepared soufflé dish. Bake for 35 minutes or until soufflé is puffed and golden. Serve with apricot or rich vanilla sauce.

Soufflé Glenfiddich

6 eggs	2–3 ounces bitter chocolate
6 ounces caster sugar	⅔ ounce crystallised fruits
3 ounces flour (sieved)	3 tablespoons whisky
⅔ pint milk	icing sugar or 1 extra table-
½ vanilla bean	spoon whisky

Separate eggs. Mix yolks well with sugar and flour. Heat milk with vanilla bean and, when it begins to boil, pour on top of egg–flour mixture, beating well to obtain a smooth paste. Pour into a double saucepan and cook until very hot. Remove immediately. Add chopped chocolate, 3 tablespoons whisky, and crystallised fruits. Cool slightly. Beat egg whites until they form peaks and fold into mixture. Butter soufflé dish generously, taking care to cover the edges so that soufflé does not stick. Sprinkle with sugar. Cook in a fairly slow oven, Gas 3/325°F, for 20 minutes. Just before serving, sprinkle soufflé with a little icing sugar and glaze under grill, or prick the top gently with a fork and sprinkle with a little whisky.

Standfast peaches

1 large tin peach halves	3 tablespoons whisky
2 tablespoons butter	large carton double cream
2 tablespoons brown sugar	

Drain peaches and place in wide pan with butter and sugar. Heat through, spooning liquid over peaches. Add whisky, spoon over again once or twice and serve with cream.

Whisky Charlotte

½ pint coffee (or use a strong infusion of instant coffee)	4 eggs
¼ pound caster sugar	6 tablespoons whisky
2 tablespoons brown sugar	4 ounces bitter chocolate
2 ounces butter	sponge fingers
	double cream

Make a syrup of sugar and whisky heated in ¼ pint water, adding the whisky at the last minute. Melt the chocolate in the coffee. Remove pan from heat and add butter, sugar, and egg yolks, mixing well. Stiffly beat egg whites and fold in. Line a mould with sponge fingers and sprinkle with the whisky syrup. Pour in the chocolate mixture. Cover with more sponge fingers and chill until firm. Turn out and serve with unsweetened whipped cream.

Whisky cream

¼ pint double cream
¼ pint single cream
¼ ounce gelatine

1 tablespoon clear honey
2 tablespoons whisky

Dissolve gelatine in 6 tablespoons water. Whip the double cream and then add single cream and keep whipping until both thicken. Gently beat the honey and whisky together and fold into the cream with the gelatine. This takes time and perseverance, but they can all be successfully blended. Pour into glasses and chill.

Whisky sponge gâteau

30 sponge fingers
6 ounces butter
4 ounces walnuts
¼ pint milk
2 eggs

2 ounces caster sugar
8 tablespoons whisky
1 medium tin peach slices
½ pint double cream
chopped pistachio nuts

Oil a 7-inch cake tin and line with greased paper. Trim sponge fingers to the depth of the tin. Beat butter until soft and white. Grate walnuts and beat into the butter. Warm milk until steaming. Separate eggs and whisk yolks until thick with the sugar. Pour gradually into the hot milk, stirring. Cool and beat into the butter mixture, a little at a time. Beat in 2 tablespoons of whisky. Mix peach juice from tin with the rest of the whisky and pour into a deep plate. Dip the flat side of each trimmed sponge cake into this and arrange round the tin, rounded side out. Cover the base with sponge fingers and add peach slices and any broken bits of sponge. Continue until tin is filled, finishing with a layer of sponge cakes. Cover with greased paper and place weights on top. Refrigerate until well chilled. Turn out and pipe with cream. Decorate with pistachio nuts.

Candied oranges

oranges   4½ ounces sugar
whisky   ¼ pint water

Slice oranges across and soak in whisky in a refrigerator for 24 hours. Prepare a caramel sauce by heating 4½ ounces sugar very slowly in a thick pan with ¼ pint water until it is dark brown in colour (but not too dark or it will taste bitter). Pour this over the oranges and replace in refrigerator until required.

CAKES AND PRESERVES

Black bun

1 pound 10 ounces plain flour	1 level teaspoon ground ginger
salt	¼ level teaspoon black pepper
8 ounces butter	1 pound 4 ounces currants
7 eggs	5 ounces honey
4 ounces whole almonds	2 tablespoons whisky
1 pound raisins	just over ¼ pint milk
1 rounded teaspoon ground cloves	

Grease a 2-pound oblong loaf tin. Sift 1 pound flour and a pinch of salt into a bowl. Rub in butter until the mixture resembles fine breadcrumbs. Beat 4 eggs and stir enough into flour to make a fairly stiff dough. Reserve ¼ dough for lid. Roll out and line tin with rest, pricking the bottom pastry layer well.

Put almonds in a pan, cover with cold water, bring to the boil, drain and skin. Chop almonds and raisins. Sift rest of flour and add a pinch of salt, cloves, ginger, and black pepper. Stir in almonds, raisins, currants and honey. Add the whisky. Beat remaining eggs with nearly all the milk, reserving a little for brushing the top of the pastry. Add beaten eggs to mixture and stir. Pack and flatten down into pastry-lined tin.

Moisten edges of pastry and cover with rolled-out reserved pastry, sealing with thumb and forefinger. Make 4 holes in top and push a skewer down through them right to the bottom of the tin. Brush the top with milk and any left-over egg. Prick all over with a fork and bake in centre of an oven preheated to Gas 4/350°F for 2 hours 15 minutes or until a warmed skewer inserted in the top comes out clean.

Cool and leave for at least 12 hours. It keeps for at least a month in double greaseproof paper and foil.

Gâteau chevalier

12 ounces plain flour	5 eggs
8 ounces butter	½ teaspoon baking powder
8 ounces caster sugar	2 tablespoons whisky
4 ounces ground almonds	citron peel

Sift flour. Cream butter and sugar and beat in almonds. Beat in each egg singly with a little of the flour. Stir in the rest of the flour with baking powder and whisky. Turn into a greased oblong tin 8 × 5 inches and lay thin slices of citron peel down the top. Bake in centre of slow oven, Gas 3/325°F for 1½ hours. Test with skewer and, if clean, cool cake in tin.

Lemon whisky cake

3 eggs and their weight in butter, caster sugar and flour	1 large lemon
	6 tablespoons whisky
	1 teaspoon baking powder
6 ounces sultanas	

(Preparations must begin the day before the cake is needed.) Pare off lemon-rind very thinly. Put it into a glass with the whisky. Do this the day before making the cake. Cream the butter, beat in the sugar until white. Separate the eggs and sift the flour. Add the yolks one at a time with a spoonful of the flour, beating thoroughly. Mix the sultanas in with the strained whisky and a little more of the flour. Whip the whites stiffly and fold into the mixture with the remaining flour and the baking powder. Turn into a greased and papered tin and bake in a moderate oven for 1–1½ hours. This mixture also makes an excellent seed-cake using a dessertspoon of caraway seeds instead of the sultanas.

Stem ginger Glenfiddich

Stem ginger is traditionally preferred by men. The gentleman who tasted the preserve described below for us said it was so delicious that it had put him right off stem ginger without whisky.

Measure out in tablespoons the amount of syrup in a jar of stem ginger. To each tablespoonful add two of whisky. Place in a bowl and marinate the ginger in the liquid overnight.

Tobermory tartlets

Pastry
½ pound plain flour
3 fluid ounces olive oil
¼ teaspoon salt
2 tablespoons cold water

Filling
6 ounces raisins
4 ounces sugar
3 eggs

1 teaspoon vanilla
2 ounces butter
6 ounces chopped walnuts
4 tablespoons whisky

Topping
caster sugar
glacé cherries
1 tablespoon whisky

Sieve flour and salt into a bowl. Add the oil and water. Mix into a firm dough. Knead lightly on a floured board and cover and chill for 10–15 minutes before rolling. Soak the raisins in whisky. Cream the butter and sugar. Stir in the beaten eggs, fruit, nuts and vanilla. Make 12 3–inch pastry cases in muffin tins and fill with the mixture. Bake at Gas 4/350°F for 40–45 minutes. Put on a wire rack to cool, and sprinkle while hot with the extra whisky. When cold, dredge with caster sugar and decorate with halved glacé cherries.

Whisky cake Valerie

1 large orange	6 ounces caster sugar
5 dessertspoons whisky	3 large eggs
6 ounces sultanas	8 ounces plain flour
6 ounces butter	pinch salt

Pare rind thinly off orange and soak in whisky for at least 6 hours. Discard the rind and add sultanas to whisky. Cream butter and sugar until light and fluffy. Beat the eggs and beat gradually into the creamed mixture. Sift the flour, salt and baking powder together and fold into the mixture, then fold in the sultanas and whisky. Spoon mixture into greased round 7-inch tin lined with greaseproof paper.

Bake for 1½ hours in centre of oven heated to Gas 4/350°F, reducing the heat towards the end of the cooking if the cake seems to be browning too much. Eat while fresh.

Whisky marmalade

1½ pounds Seville oranges	2 lemons
2 small ordinary oranges	3 pounds granulated sugar
(½ pound in all)	4 tablespoons whisky

Cut up all peel with a sharp knife, removing all pith and shredding the rest. Keep all pith, pips and juice in a separate bowl. Wash 5 1-pound jars and drain dry, then put them in a very low oven to warm through. Squeeze out any extra fruit juice. Tie pips, pith and any left-overs in muslin. Put this bag into a pan with fruit juice and 4 pints water.

Cook over a slow heat for 1½ hours. By then the liquid should have been reduced to 3 pints. If it looks like more, then go on cooking. It is also essential to make sure the peel is really cooked, otherwise the result will be very tough. Now remove the muslin bag, add the sugar, stir until dissolved, and do *not* leave marmalade unattended. Boil rapidly for about 15 minutes, then try for 'setting'.

Testing: Put a little marmalade on to a cold saucer. Leave for a few minutes in the fridge, then push with a teaspoon to see if it wrinkles. If it doesn't, boil a little longer and then test again.

When setting-point is reached, stir in the whisky and let the pan stand for 15 minutes before filling warmed jars. Seal with special 'jam' circle, cover, and elastic band.

IX

WHISKY AND WHAT?

'We'll mak' our maut, we'll brew our drink,
We'll dance, and sing, and rejoice, man;
And mony braw thanks to the meikle black de'il
That danced awa' wi' th' Exciseman.'
'The De'il's Awa' Wi' Th' Exciseman', ROBERT BURNS

WITH the mellow spread of Scotch into areas never reached before, it is becoming increasingly realised that this is a robust and versatile spirit which lends itself admirably to mixing with other drinks. The diehard traditionalists will always, and correctly, take their straight malts neat or with not more than an equal quantity of water—preferably Malvern, Appolinaris, Vichy, Evian, Vittel, or Pellegrino—but as there is now a vast range of excellent blends available, and convention has slackened its hold on popular taste, the enterprising drinker can experiment with a variety of interesting new sensations which still owe their inspiration to Scotch proper.

Customs change as the economy changes, and the man-in-the-street makes the final choice of what he wants to drink and how he intends to drink it. In the 'twenties and up until the war the Scotsman's favourite drink, when he could afford it, was the chaser—a dram taken neat and followed by a beer in one single flowing and beautifully executed movement. The object was to paralyse the cortex and stun the medulla oblongata as quickly as possible. Today more often than not he dilutes his whisky with fizzy lemonade. The young executive, influenced by American business methods, has taken to Scotch on the rocks, a blend stultified with frozen tap-water rendered fairly germ-proof by the addition of chlorine. At the gentlemen-only clubs around St James's the call is still for a sedate whisky and soda. But with money circulating faster, and because women have become more mobile in society, the cocktails and exotic mixed drinks of an earlier age are back in public acclaim.

Obviously one would not make a cocktail with a Glenfiddich pure malt nor with a truly de luxe blend, but a fine blended whisky like Grant's goes splendidly with amalgams of fruits and liquors as well as with cocktails of every sort. In the list which follows, a few whisky mixes were evolved from a base of Scotch, where others, originally connected with Irish or Bourbon, can equally well—or better—be made with Scotch. Some of the drinks given are historically associated with gin, such as the Collins and Rickey, but they have become mutated and may these days equally be founded on Scotch whisky. Again, drinks like a Sangaree have a vinous connection, but many of the accepted authorities offer spirituous versions.

The trouble with virtually all mixed drinks is that no two authorities will give precisely the same recipe; in fact, in certain instances they may differ infuriatingly, or give so many variations on a theme that it takes considerable knowledge to choose which will be acceptable to one's mood at the time. For instance, the most erudite of mix-masters, David E. Embury, in *The Fine Art of Mixing Drinks*, gives four different basic Manhattans, for which he stipulates that five different spirits, including Scotch, are permissible.

We are indebted to Mr Embury, and also to John Doxat for his first-rate paperback, *Booth's Handbook of Cocktails and Mixed Drinks*, and his much larger *Drinks and Drinking*. Recourse in settling argument, and seeking compromise and confirmation, has also been had from *Trader Vic's Bartender's Guide*, *The Savoy Cocktail Book*, *Scotch Whisky: Questions and Answers* and *The International Guide to Drinks* (edited by John Doxat and published by the United Kingdom Bartenders' Guild, but not, unfortunately, available to non-members).

We have given recipes that are simple, complex, long, short, and a few that are admittedly anachronistic curiosities. A 'measure' means a jigger of one fluid ounce, the '5-out' of British commerce.

Before the amateur drink-mixer studies the following recipes, some explanatory notes are necessary.

Drink mixes are normally in the proportion of *one drink only*. Thus they must be augmented according to how many you want to make. This does not apply to punches, however. A good example is Whisky Cup (page 105), in which it will be obvious that two bottles of whisky is more than enough for one person.

Cocktail recipes usually mention 'powdered sugar'. This means caster sugar.

You 'crack' ice by putting it into a clean towel and either banging it on a hard surface or hitting it with a hammer.

'Sugar syrup' is made by boiling 1 pound of sugar slowly in 1 pint of water. It can then be bottled and stored in the fridge.

You 'squeeze' rind by pinching it in your fingers. It should *never* be forced through a fruit-press.

Only the really professional drink-mixer worries too much about glasses. You need tall glasses for some drinks, short glasses for others. If you really want 'Old-Fashioned' glasses, then any large china-and-glass shop or department will know what you mean if you ask for them by name. But the best all-purpose container is the legless 'dumpy' tumbler containing 4–5 fluid ounces. These may be obtained very cheaply.

Finally, drink recipes are essentially guide-lines, not necessarily to be followed slavishly but geared to personal experience and preferences.

DRINKS

Atholl brose

whisky   honey
oatmeal   cream

Use personal taste as to proportions of whisky well mixed with finely ground oatmeal, honey and cream. Leave to stand and 'meld' for a time before serving.

There is also a cocktail version: 2 measures whisky, a measure each of honey and single cream. Mix in warmed glass and allow to cool. Or, as a toddy, omit the cream and top with hot milk.

Barbary Coast

half-measure orange juice   2 measures whisky
half-measure red vermouth   dash of yellow Chartreuse

Shake with cracked ice, strain into a stemmed glass, and decorate with a slice of orange peel, twisted.

A version of this, or the same name (but perhaps better called a Barbarous Coast) calls for a measure of *crème de cacao*, 2 measures each of gin and whisky, and a tablespoon of double cream.

Blood and sand

1 measure whisky   1 measure orange juice
1 measure cherry brandy   1 measure red vermouth

Shake with ice and strain into a small wine goblet.

Bobby Burns

2 measures whisky   1 teaspoon Benedictine
1 measure red vermouth

Shake with ice and strain into a small wine goblet. Squeeze lemon rind over but do not put in the drink.

Brooklyn

half-measure dry vermouth   2 dashes maraschino and
2 measures whisky   Amer Picon (or angostura)

Stir with ice cubes in Old-Fashioned glass. A variation of the Manhattan (page 99).

Buck

¼ lemon   ginger ale
2 measures whisky

Squeeze juice of a quarter lemon into a tall glass and then throw in the squeezed fruit. Add several cubes and 2 measures whisky. Top with ginger ale.

Bunny hug

1 measure whisky   1 measure gin
1 measure pernod

Shake with ice and strain into a small wine goblet.

Buster Brown

A Sour (page 103) plus a dash of orange bitters.

Churchill

A Manhattan (page 99) plus a dash of lime juice (or lemon juice) and a dash of Cointreau.

Cobbler

1 measure maraschino,	whisky
Cointreau or sugar syrup	pineapple chunks

A hundred years ago this was thought to be the most popular mixed drink in the U.S.A. when made with sherry. To make the whisky version, nearly fill a tall glass with crushed ice, pour in a measure of maraschino or Cointreau, or simple sugar syrup. Add plenty of whisky, stir with a bar spoon until the glass is well frosted. Decorate with pineapple chunks or similar fruit, and serve with straws.

Collins

Originally a gin drink—and arguably the single most popular mix nationally in the U.S.A.—the Collins is fairly widely made with whisky.

1 measure whisky	$\frac{1}{2}$ tablespoon powdered sugar
juice of $\frac{1}{2}$ lemon	soda water

Pour over ice cubes in a tumbler, stir, and top with soda water.
  A Whisky Collins (with Scotch) is sometimes called a Sandy Collins, and John Doxat says that in parts of Australia this is known as a Peter Collins.

Cooler

lemon rind	soda water
2 measures whisky	

Place rind of a whole lemon in a tall glass with ice cubes, 2 measures of whisky, and top up with soda water.

Country club

A Whisky Cocktail (page 105) made with both angostura and orange or peach bitters.

Crusta

lemon or orange rind
powdered sugar
½ measure sugar syrup
1 measure lemon juice

2 dashes maraschino and
   angostura
2 measures whisky

Cut the rind from a large lemon or a small orange in one continuous spiral. Line a large wine goblet with this. Dampen edge of glass and dip in powdered sugar. Mix, separately, a ½ measure of sugar syrup, 1 measure lemon juice, couple of dashes of maraschino and angostura, 2 measures whisky, and ice. Shake well and strain into the previously prepared goblet.

Daisy

½ measure grenadine (or sugar
   syrup)
1 measure lime or lemon juice

3 measures whisky
fruit to decorate

Shake with ice a ½ measure of grenadine (or sugar syrup), 1 measure of lime (or lemon) juice, 3 measures whisky. Pour into a goblet nearly filled with crushed ice. Decorate with any fruit you fancy, and serve with straws.

Fix

Virtually the same as a Daisy (see previous recipe), but some say that maraschino or Cointreau should be substituted for grenadine. Some also say that a Daisy should be languidly pink, from the grenadine, and a fix should be white. But these drinks are at least a century old and the recipes blurred by the years.

Fizz

1 measure whisky	½ tablespoonful powdered
juice of ½ lemon	sugar

Shake well with ice, strain into stemmed goblet and top with soda water.

Frisco

1 measure Benedictine	2 measures whisky
½ measure lemon juice	

Shake with cracked ice and strain into a cocktail glass.

Grant's cooler

1 measure whisky	apple juice
2 tablespoons concentrated	orange slice
orange juice	

Put 1 measure whisky into a tall glass with ice cubes. Add 2 tablespoons concentrated orange juice and top up with apple juice. Garnish the side of the glass with a whole slice of orange, cut so that it fits neatly over the edge.

Highball

This originally meant a tall, usually whisky, unflavoured spirit drink in the U.S.A.—as opposed to, say, a Julep. It is now indiscriminately used for various long iced spirit drinks topped with mineral or plain water.

Horse's neck

lemon rind	ginger ale
2 measures whisky	

Peel a lemon in a continuous spiral and hang the rind from the rim of a tall glass. Put in several ice cubes and 2 measures of whisky and top with ginger ale (dry or American according to preference).

Julep

There is no reason why this should not be made with Scotch whisky, but it is very strongly associated with Bourbon—though we might remind ourselves that the word 'julep' is Persian in origin! There is much dispute in 'mixing' circles as to the correct method of preparation, so we give here a simple one that has excellent authority behind it.

'Muddle' four sprigs of fresh mint with a lump of sugar and a little water in a tall glass. Fill with cracked ice. Add at least 2 measures of whisky, garnish with a sprig of mint, and do not stir.

Lafayette

Another Manhattan (*see below*) with Dubonnet in place of vermouth.

Loch Lomond

1½ measures whisky   2 dashes angostura
1 teaspoon sugar syrup

Shake 1½ measures whisky, 1 teaspoon sugar syrup and 2 dashes angostura and strain into a cocktail glass.

Manhattan

This classic and ubiquitous 'cocktail' has weathered the passage of time since Harry Johnson, 'publisher and bartender', first put out in New York his illustrated *Bartenders' Manual, or How to Mix Drinks of the Present Style* in 1882—long before the so-called Cocktail Age of the 1920–37 period.

We refer to various so-called 'Manhattans' and so we feel it might be well to give the authentic recipe hereunder.

1 measure Bourbon whiskey	½ measure sweet vermouth
½ measure dry vermouth	dash of angostura

Stir, strain into a cocktail glass, and serve with a cocktail cherry.

Milk punch

1 egg	2 teaspoons sugar syrup
½ pint milk	2 measures whisky

Shake a whole egg, ½ pint milk, 2 teaspoons sugar syrup, and 2 measures whisky with crushed ice until well chilled. Strain into a goblet and top with grated nutmeg.

Millionaire

A version of Ward Eight (page 104) omitting the fruit juice and using a measure of Cointreau and a little egg white. In the U.S.A. there are further regional mutations of this drink.

New Deal

½ measure sugar syrup	3 measures whisky
1 measure Amer Picon	

Stir with ice in an Old-Fashioned glass and add a twisted slice of orange peel.

New York

2 measures whisky	1 heaped teaspoon powdered
1 teaspoon unsweetened lime juice	sugar

Briskly stir ingredients, strain into a cocktail glass, and squeeze lemon rind over.

Old-fashioned

1 teaspoon sugar syrup   1½ measures whisky
3 dashes angostura

Some claim that this drink may only be made with American whiskey, but to designate Scotch is now perfectly in order. In a small tumbler (the dumpy type that takes its name from this cocktail) put 1 teaspoon sugar syrup, 3 dashes angostura, 2 ice cubes and 1½ measures whisky. Stir well, serve with stirrer, and add a twist of lemon rind and a cocktail cherry.

Rickey

2 measures whisky   1 teaspoon grenadine
1 lime   soda water

Over ice in a tumbler pour 2 measures of whisky, juice of half a fresh lime and a teaspoon of grenadine. Add the entire squeezed lime and top with soda water.

    The name of this drink is said to have come from 'Colonel Jim' Rickey, whose real name was Joe and who was certainly not a colonel. He was a well-known Congress lobbyist at the beginning of this century and frequented Shoemaker's restaurant in Washington D.C. The bartender invented the first experimental 'rickey', using gin, for 'Colonel Jim', who adopted it as his daily tipple from then on.

Rob Roy

½ measure whisky   ½ measure sweet vermouth

Shake ½ measure whisky and ⅓ measure sweet vermouth and strain into a cocktail glass.

Rusty nail

A measure of whisky and Drambuie served 'on the rocks'.

St Moritz

Another version of the ever-popular Manhattan (page 99) plus
pineapple juice in equal measure to the vermouth employed.

Sangaree

2 teaspoons sugar syrup   grated nutmeg
2 measures whisky

In a tall glass over ice cubes put 2 teaspoons sugar syrup, 2
measures whisky, top with water and dust with grated nutmeg.

Sazerac

1 teaspoon sugar syrup   2 dashes Pernod
3 dashes angostura bitters   lemon peel
2 measures whisky

Fill an Old-Fashioned glass with crushed ice. Mix separately
with a little more ice a teaspoon of sugar syrup, 3 dashes angostura bitters, and 2 measures whisky. Empty well-chilled Old-
Fashioned glass and put in a couple of dashes of Pernod. Twist
this around to coat the glass and then pour in the mixture and
a twist of lemon peel.

This may also be made with a ½ measure red vermouth, 3
measures whisky, a dash of Pernod, and stirred with ice in an
Old-Fashioned glass.

The name 'Sazerac' also applies to a proprietary American
bottled cocktail.

Scotch mist

lemon peel   2 measures whisky

Firmly squeeze a long strip of lemon peel over crushed ice in
a shaker. Then drop the rind in, add 2 measures whisky, and
shake vigorously. Pour the lot into an Old-Fashioned glass.

Shake

Effectively, a Sour (*see below*) with less lemon juice.

Sling

1 teaspoon sugar syrup   3 measures whisky
2 teaspoons lemon juice   dash angostura

Mix with ice in a tall glass 1 teaspoon sugar syrup, 2 teaspoons lemon juice, 3 measures whisky, and a dash of angostura. Top with soda water or ginger ale.

    For the hot version use boiling water and a little powdered cinnamon.

Sour

1 measure whisky   juice of ½ lemon
½ teaspoon powdered sugar   1 teaspoon egg white

Shake together 1 measure whisky, ½ teaspoon powdered sugar, juice of ½ lemon, and a teaspoon of egg white. Strain into a large cocktail glass.

    Another version omits egg white and tops drink with a squirt of soda water.

Squirt

1 peach   1 teaspoon Cointreau
1 tablespoon sugar syrup   1 measure whisky

Crush a fresh peach in a mixing glass. Add a tablespoon of sugar syrup, a teaspoon of Cointreau, and a measure of whisky. Shake with crushed ice, strain into a tall glass and top with soda water.

Swizzle

A Sour (page 103) without the egg white. The drink is agitated in its glass with a swizzle-stick (hence the name) until it becomes frothy. Leave this mixture to get cold in the refrigerator before straining it into glasses.

Toddy

1 teaspoon sugar   whisky
boiling water

Heap a teaspoon of sugar in a warm glass. Add a little boiling water to dissolve. Add 2 measures whisky and stir with a silver spoon. Pour in more boiling water and top with more whisky to taste.

Toronto

2 measures whisky   4 dashes angostura bitters

Over ice cubes in an Old-Fashioned glass pour 2 measures of whisky and add 4 dashes angostura bitters (and, optionally, a few dashes of Cointreau). Stir, and decorate with a slice of lemon rind.

Trinity

Again, a Manhattan (page 99). This time with a dash of orange bitters, apricot bitters and crème de menthe. (The complexities of drink-mixing are well illustrated here. A Trinity is also an entirely different gin cocktail.)

Ward eight

½ measure grenadine   ½ measure orange juice
1 measure lemon juice   3 measures whisky

Shake with cracked ice and pour the lot into a tall glass. Top with soda water, add fruit as available, and serve with straws.

Whisky cocktail

2 measures whisky   4 dashes angostura bitters

Over large ice cubes in an Old-Fashioned glass pour 2 measures whisky and add 4 dashes angostura bitters (and a few dashes of Cointreau optionally). Stir, and decorate with a slice of lemon rind.

Whisky cup

2 pounds strawberries
¼ pint crushed pineapple
¾ pound powdered sugar
¾ bottle dark rum
1 pint lemon juice
½ pint grenadine (or sugar syrup)
2 bottles whisky
1 quart ginger ale

In a large bowl put 2 pounds strawberries, ¼ pint of crushed pineapple (preferably fresh), ¾ pound powdered sugar, and ¾ bottle of dark rum. Cover and leave for about 12 hours. Add 1 pint of lemon juice (canned, unsweetened will do), ½ pint of grenadine (or sugar syrup), and 2 bottles of whisky. Mix and pour over ice cubes in a punch bowl. Add a quart of ginger ale and a siphon of soda water.

Whisky Mac

Half-and-half whisky and ginger wine. Do not ice.

Zoom

Shake very vigorously with crushed ice proportions of 1 honey, 2 double cream and 6 whisky.

In addition to those drinks we have already detailed there are the following which appear in *Scotch Whisky, Questions and Answers*, obtainable from the Scotch Whisky Association, Edinburgh.

Derby fizz

5 dashes lemon juice   3 dashes curaçao
1 teaspoon powdered sugar   1 glass whisky
1 egg   soda water

Earthquake

one-third gin   one-third absinthe
one-third whisky

Flying Scotsman

2½ glasses Italian vermouth   1 tablespoon bitters
3 glasses whisky   1 tablespoon sugar syrup

Highland coffee

Whisky, hot coffee, brown sugar and cream to taste.

Highland cooler

1 teaspoon powdered sugar   1 glass whisky
juice of ½ lemon   1 lump ice
2 dashes angostura   ginger ale

Highland special

3 glasses whisky   ½ glass orange juice
2 glasses French vermouth

Add a little nutmeg after mixing.

Scotch Tom Collins

5–6 dashes lemon   2–3 lumps ice
1 large glass whisky

Pour into a large glass and fill with soda.

Summer Scotch

1 glass whisky	1 lump ice
3 dashes crème de menthe	

Fill up glass with soda.

Whisper

2 glasses whisky	2 glasses Italian vermouth
2 glasses French vermouth	cracked ice

Whisky and water?
One man's views on the pros and cons of diluting whisky:

How, when and where do you drink a single malt? First of all, I contend that it should be drunk neat with, if desired, a chaser afterwards. It is a sin to adulterate it with soda, dry ginger or even plain water unless that water is the genuine soft Scottish water from the Highland streams. The best time to drink it is in the evening, after dinner, and as a liqueur, when you have plenty of time to sit back and enjoy it. As a hurried aperitif in a noisy, smoky atmosphere you do not get the full advantage. On the other hand, I am not one of those who like to surround the consumption of wines and spirits with a lot of ritual, mumbo jumbo or whatever you like to call it, so I would rather have it under unfavourable conditions than not at all.

Jack Mahoney

X

A WHISKY MISCELLANY

'We are na fou, we're nae that fou,
But just a drappie in our e'e;
The cock may craw, the day may daw',
And aye we'll taste the barley bree.'
'O, Willie Brewed a Peck o' Maut', ROBERT BURNS

THE Worshipful Company of Distillers is one of the ancient guild companies of the City of London. Its chosen motto is 'Droppe as Raine distill as Dewe'. The Company was founded in 1638 by Sir Theodore de Mayerne, physician to Charles I, and Dr Thomas Cadman, physician to the Queen. Sir Theodore died from drinking bad wine in a tavern in the Strand. *Quod erat downthestrandum*, if one may say so.

Over 78 per cent of all Scotch whisky is consumed in foreign markets.

The first Coffey still was established at Port Dundas, near Glasgow, in about 1840. Blending did not begin until twenty years later.

The Scotch Whisky Association was formed in 1942 and incorporated in 1960. The aims of the Association are: to protect and promote the interests of the industry at home and abroad; to originate, promote, support or oppose legislative or other measures directly or indirectly affecting the industry; to enter into legal proceedings in any part of the world in defence of the interests of the industry; to collect statistical and other information relating to the industry and to supply members with such information.

The Spey is the fastest-flowing river in Britain. It is obvious that running swiftly ensures purity. A pity Caesar's wife didn't know this.

Everything that comes from Scotland in fact or by nomenclature is called *Scottish* except Scotch whisky, which is *Scotch*. Allowable variations might be Scotch tweed, Scotch egg, Scotch beef, Scotch Corner in the north of England—or, in army parlance, Scotch mist.

Grain whisky costs roughly half as much to produce as pot-still malt whisky, and a patent-still yields more whisky in a month than a pot-still yields in a year.

'Macdonald, one of our actors in Bass's troupe, Dundee, always carried a large-sized bamboo cane, at all times his companion. We were crossing the river Tay in a ferry-boat from Dundee, careworn, hungry, and tired; no money, salaries unpaid; yet Jemmy Macdonald seemed little to feel it. There came no repinings from him; this was a riddle to us starvelings. Aboard the boat he whispered to me: "Laddie, come abaft." *Sotto voce.* "Not a word, laddie," unscrewing his bamboo, the top a cup, the stick a whiskey bottle. "Tak' a drink, laddie—real Glenlivat; nae excise-man ever took gauge of this whiskey." This I believe; it was I don't know what above proof. In the stick lay "Jemmy's" hilarity. Doubtless many of us find comfort in the stick at times.' (From *Old Drury Lane*, fifty years' recollections of author, actor and manager. Edward Stirling, 1881.)

In the distillery business no machine has yet been invented that can take the place of the trained nose.

Statistics show that moderate drinkers have a greater expectation of life than teetotallers. A jollier one too.

O. Henry wrote of whisky in *The Lost Blend*: 'It gives men courage and ambition and the nerve for anything. It has the colour of gold, is as clear as glass and shines after dark as if the sunshine were still in it.'

'Some of the Highland Gentlemen are Immoderate Drinkers of Usky, even three or four Quarts at a Sitting; and in general, the People that can pay the Purchase, drink it without Moderation.

Not long ago, four English Officers took a Fancy to try their Strength in this Bow of Ulysses, against a like Number of the Country Champions, but the Enemy came off victorious; and one of the Officers was thrown into a Fit of the Gout, without Hopes; another had a most dangerous Fever, a third lost his Skin and Hair by the Surfeit, and the last confessed to me, that when Drunkenness and Debate ran high, he took several Opportunities to sham it.' (*Letters from a Gentleman in the North of Scotland to his Friend in London*, 1754.)

There is a saying in the Highlands: 'One whisky is all right, two is too much, and three is too few.'

'The cheer she [Mrs Macintosh, "a tidy guid-wife"] offered us was never more than bread and cheese and whisky ... the whisky was a bad habit, there was certainly too much of it going. At every house it was offered, at every house it must be tested or offence would be given, so we were taught to believe. I am sure now that had we steadily refused compliance with so incorrect a custom it would have been far better for ourselves, and might all the sooner have put a stop to so pernicious a habit among the people. Whisky-drinking was and is the bane of that country; from early morning till late at night it went on. Decent gentlewomen began the day with a dram. In our house the bottle of whisky, with its accompaniment of a silver salver full of small glasses, was placed on the side-table with cold meat every morning. In the pantry a bottle of whisky was the allowance per day, with bread and cheese in any required quantity, for such messengers or visitors whose errands sent them in that direction. The very poorest cottages could offer whisky; all the men engaged in the wood manufacture drank it in goblets three times a day, yet except at a merry-making we never saw any one tipsy.' (Elizabeth Grant of Rothiemurchas, early nineteenth century.)

The best oak for maturing whisky is American white oak from the United States. Sherry casks from Arkansas oak often reach Scotland from America via Spain.

'Madam, I dare say that this is the first epistle you ever received from this nether world. I write you from the regions of Hell, amid the horrors of the damn'd. The time and manner of my leaving your earth I do not exactly know, as I took my departure in the heat of a fever of intoxication, contracted at your too hospitable mansion; but, on my arrival here, I was fairly tried, and sentenced to endure the purgatorial tortures of this infernal confine for the space of ninety-nine years, eleven months, and twenty-nine days, and all on account of the impropriety of my conduct yesternight under your roof. Here am I, laid on a bed of pitiless furze, with my aching head reclined on a pillow of ever-piercing thorn, while an infernal tormentor, wrinkled, and old, and cruel, his name I think is *Recollection*, with a whip of scorpions, forbids peace or rest to approach me, and keeps anguish eternally awake. Still, Madam, if I could in any measure be reinstated in the good opinion of the fair circle whom my conduct last night as much injured, I think it would be an alleviation of my torments. For this reason I trouble you with this letter. To the men of the company I will make no apology— Your husband, who insisted on my drinking more than I chose, has no right to blame me; and the other gentlemen were partakers of my guilt. But to you, Madam, I have much to apologize. Your good opinion I valued as one of the greatest acquisitions I had made on earth, and I was truly a beast to forfeit it. There was a Miss I . . . too, a woman of fine sense, gentle and unassuming manners—do make, on my part, a miserable damn'd wretch's best apology to her. A Mrs G . . ., a charming woman, did me the honour to be prejudiced in my favour; this makes me hope that I have not outraged her beyond all forgiveness. To all the other ladies please present my humblest contrition for my conduct, and my petition for their gracious pardon. Of all ye powers of decency and decorum! whisper to them that my errors, though great, were involuntary—that an intoxicated man is the vilest of beasts—that it was not in my nature to be brutal to anyone—that to be rude to a woman, when in my senses, was impossible with me—but—Regret! Remorse! Shame! ye three hellhounds that ever dog my steps and bay at my heels, spare me! spare me! spare me!

> Forgive the offences, and pity the perdition of, Madam,
>
> > Your humble Slave,
> >
> > (Robt. Burns)'

(Letter to Mrs Robert Riddell, 1793, from the poet Robert Burns.) What did he *do*?!

In one year Scotch earned over £109 million from sales in the U.S.A., taking 50 per cent of the total output. The other main markets, listed alphabetically here, are Australia, Belgium, Canada, France, Italy, Japan, South Africa, Spain, and West Germany. The largest growing export market is Italy.

The despairing and sickly feeling called a hangover is in fact alcoholic gastritis exacerbated by oxygen starvation and dehydration. The following are three prescribed cures. They do not work.

As far back as 1594, Sir Hugh Plat, in *The Jewell House of Art and Nature*, more suspicious of wine than whisky, advocates the taking in of oleaginous ballast before the event. 'Drinke first a good large draught of Sallet Oyle, for that will floate upon the wine which you shall drinke, and suppresse the spirites from ascending into the braine. Also what quantitie soever of newe milk you drinke first you may drinke thrise as much wine after, without danger of being drunke. But howe

sicke you shall bee with this prevention, I will not here deter-
mine, neither woulde I have set downe this experiment, but
openly for the helpe of such modest drinkers as sometimes in
companie are drawne, or rather forced to pledge in full bolles
such quaffing companions as they would be loth to offend, and
will require reason at their hands as they term it.'

George Smith, writing in 1738, put his faith in an astounding
potion he thoughtfully called 'surfeit-water'. 'Take Centuary,
Marigold-flowers, Mint, Rosemary, Mugwort, Scordium, Rue,
Carduus, Balm, Dragons, St John's Wort, each two handfuls;
roots of Angelica, Butter-bur, Piony, Scorzonera, each seven
ounces; Calmous Aromaticus, Galingal, Angelica-seeds, Cara-
ways each ten drachms, Ginger six drachms, red Poppy-flowres
three handfuls; proof spirits three gallons; water one gallon
and a half; macerate, distil and dulcify with fine Sugar, one
pound and a half for use.'

As Douglas Sutherland—in whose *Raise Your Glasses* I found
this—says, there is no indication of how many hangovers this
vast concoction was expected to cure, but unless the compound-
ing had been done well in advance of the night out, even the
worst hangover would have disappeared before the mixture was
ready for the first shuddering mouthful.

A much simpler remedy was suggested in *Medical Experi-
ments, 1692–94*, by the Hon. Robert Boyle. 'Take green Hem-
lock that is tender, and put it in your socks, so that it may lie
thinly between them and the Soles of your Feet; shift the Herbs
once a day.'

And with this, I think we can be said to have covered the
subject from head to foot.

When replacing an old still with a new one, cautious distillers
have been known to 'damage' or dent the new still to make its
shape the same as the original 'in case it might affect the flavour
of the whisky' if they didn't.

The entire stocks of Scotch whisky held in this country at the
time of writing exceed 867,000,000 proof gallons.

Neil Gunn, author of *Whisky and Scotland*, who like Robert Burns before him had been an excise officer, had this to say about malt whiskies: 'These generous whiskies with their individual flavours, recall the world of hills and glens, of raging elements, of shelter, of divine ease. The perfect moment of their reception is after arduous bodily stress—or mental stress, if the body be sound. The essential oils that wind in the glass then uncurl their long fingers in lingering benediction and the noble works of creation are made manifest. At such a moment the basest man would bless his enemy.'

Towards the end of her reign, Queen Victoria gave orders that a full bottle of whisky was to be put in a certain cupboard every night for the exclusive use of her servant John Brown. It is said that the practice went on long after his death and only ceased shortly after the accession of Queen Elizabeth II. The cupboard must indeed have been a large one.

A recent survey of Scotch drinkers has shown that 8 per cent of men and 9 per cent of women, mainly Scots, prefer to dilute their whisky with lemonade. 30 per cent of men take it neat, 26 per cent with ginger ale, 22 per cent with water, and 9 per cent with soda. 33 per cent of all women like their Scotch with ginger ale.

'My habits are changing, I think i.e. from drunk to sober. Whether I shall be happier or not remains to be proved. I shall certainly be more happy in a morning; but whether I shall not sacrifice the fat, and the marrow, and the kidneys, i.e. the night, glorious care-drowning night, that heals all our wrongs, pours wine into our mortifications, changes the scene from indifferent and flat to bright and brilliant! O Manning, if I should have formed a diabolical resolution, by the time you come to England, of not admitting any spirituous liquors into my house, will you be my guest on such shameworthy terms? Is life, with such limitations, worth trying? The truth is, that my liquors bring a nest of friendly harpies about my house, who consume me.'

(Charles Lamb to Thomas Manning, 24 September 1802.) Obviously a Lamb to the slaughter.

Aeneas Macdonald, writing in 1736, quotes an exciseman as saying: 'The ruddy complexion, nimbleness and strength of these [Scots] people is not owing to water-drinking but to the aqua vitae, a malt spirit which serves for both victual and drink.'

Classically, alcohol is stated to promote sexual desire but according to Shakespeare it reduces the performance. To one act, one presumes.

'This year [1631] five Aldermen of Macclesfield met at a tavern, and drank excessively of sack and aqua vitae, three of them died the next day, and the other two were dangerously sick. Oh that drunkards would learn to be wise.' (E. D. Burghall, Vicar of Acton.)

There is some evidence to show that coronary thrombosis is more common in abstainers.

A publication called The Mirror, told in 1824 of a Highland chieftain who was advised to put small shot in his bumper glass to diminish by degrees its capacity for holding whisky, and thus to wean himself from drinking. It goes on to describe what it calls a trick worth two of this. 'Take one tea-spoonful of the tincture of columba, one tea-spoonful of the tincture of cascarilla, one tea-spoonful of the compound tincture of gentian, a wine-glass full of infusion of quassia, and twenty drops of elixir of vitriol; mix and take twice or thrice daily, and have a jug of cold water dashed over the head every morning on coming out of bed, and the feet bathed in warm water every night.' This, The Mirror insists, will positively remove the urge to tipple. It will also clearly remove the offender with the offence.

All Highland whiskies are good, some are subtly better than others, but the best are known to the Trade as 'crackerjacks'.

The recognised whiskies of the world are as follows: Scotch whisky, Irish whiskey, American whiskey (Bourbon), Australian whisky, Canadian whisky, Spanish whisky, Japanese whisky, and Chilean whisky from imported vatted malts. The insertion of an 'e' in the American and Irish spelling and its omission for Scotch and Canadian is comparatively recent, most dictionaries giving both. As late as 1909 in a report by the Royal Commission on *Whiskey and other Potable Spirits* the 'e' is used throughout, regardless of whether the reference is to Scotland or Ireland.

There is no foundation to the superstition that whisky should never be drunk with oysters. It is, in any case, pleasanter to drink it with people.

Anyone may become a whisky distiller by applying for a licence and paying the annual duty of £15·75—but only if the plant is large enough and is approved by the excise authorities.

Contrary to popular belief, a consumer on licensed premises does not have the right to see the bottle from which his drink is poured. If, however, he is shown the bottle and is unable to see it he may be liable to arrest.

Possibly the purest water sent out of Scotland for drinking with Scotch comes from Loch Katrine.

Stephen Potter on the shape of things to drink: 'It is undoubtedly the three-corneredness of the bottle which gives Grant's Scotch that muscular flavour, which is at the same time supple and yielding, though some claim that its characteristic "soopleness", if not its yieldingness, is at least partially ascribable to the whisky itself.'

If whiskies from different distilleries are said to be of similar distinction they are known as 'kissing cousins'.

The highest village in Scotland is Wanlockhead. No doubt it sometimes sobers up.

An early writer, quoted in Grant's *Focus* magazine, reports the findings of an extoller of the Virtues of Whisky as follows: 'He distinguisheth three sorts thereof—Simplex, Composita, Perfectissima . . . Beying moderatelie taken, saith he, it sloweth age, it strengtheneth youth, it quickeneth the spirites, it cureth the hydropsie, it healeth the strangury, it pounceth the stone, it repelleth gravel, it puffeth away ventositie, it kepyth and preserveth the head from whirling—the guts from rumbling—the hands from shivering—the sinoews from shrinking—the veynes from crumpling—the bones from aking—the marrow from soaking—and trulie it is a sovereign liquor if it be orderlie taken.'

Just as we've always said.

Bibliography

Robert Burns: *The Poetical Works of Robert Burns* (Frederick Warne, London)

David Daiches: *Scotch Whisky: Its Past and Present* (André Deutsch, London)

John Doxat: *Booth's Handbook of Cocktails and Mixed Drinks* (Pan, London)

John Doxat: *Drinks and Drinking* (Ward Lock. London)

David E. Embury: *The Fine Art of Mixing Drinks* (Faber, London)

Sir Robert Bruce-Lockhart: *Scotch* (Putnam, London)

R. J. S. McDowell: *The Whiskies of Scotland* (John Murray, London)

Matty Simmons: *The Diners' Club Drink Book* (Lancer Books, New York)

Douglas Sutherland: *Raise Your Glasses* (MacDonald, London)

Rowland Watson: *Merry Gentlemen* (T. Werner Laurie, London)

Ross Wilson: *Scotch* (Constable, London)

Esquire's The Art of Mixing Drinks (Bantam, London)

The Savoy Cocktail Book (Constable, London)

Scotch Whisky: Questions and Answers (The Scotch Whisky Association, Edinburgh)

Trader Vic's Bartenders' Guide (Garden City Books, New York)

Index of Recipes

75P

To Doug. and Jenny.
Happy Christmas 1976.
Love from Gill, David
Ross and Ewan.
xxxx.